INTROVATIVE

THE INTROVERT'S INNOVATIVE PLAYBOOK

7 Steps to Accelerate Your Career Success

ROHIT R. CHOWDHRY

**(Author of the acclaimed book
"How to Get into Your Goldilocks Zone")**

notionpress.com

INDIA · SINGAPORE · MALAYSIA

Advance praise from the Field
INTROVATIVE

An Introvert's Career Compass to Navigate Success Authentically:

"This book is a powerful tool for any introvert ready to alter their career trajectory. INTROVATIVE by Rohit Chowdhry dispels myths about introversion with compelling research and provides a robust framework for building a successful career path that does not compel one to change their inherent nature. It's about time the corporate world recognizes the unique capabilities introverts bring to the table. Every introvert should read INTROVATIVE to discover their path to success and self-advocacy in the workplace."

– Dr. Annurag Batra
Entrepreneur, Author, Angel investor, TV show host.
(Founder and Editor in Chief of exchange4media, managing several big names under its aegis. Chairman and Editor in Chief of BW Businessworld Media Group, one of the most respected business publications in the country. Appointed by Government of India as the Chairman of an industry committee)

Empowering Inclusivity in the Workplace:

"INTROVATIVE goes beyond personal development to advocate for systemic change in how workplaces embrace introversion. This book is a coaching program for introverts on their career paths. The chapter on creating an introvert-friendly environment speaks to a broader audience, offering a blueprint for inclusivity and diversity in the corporate landscape. This book is an essential read for leaders and organizations committed to fostering a culture of understanding and empowerment."

– Kamalakar Sai Palavalasa
Founder & Group CEO – MicroNsure, India

Leadership is Not about Being the Loudest:

"Through this book, Rohit has attempted to provide a blueprint for introverts to not only survive but thrive in the corporate world. This book is a companion for introverts aiming to carve their path to success in the workplace. It meticulously addresses every facet of professional challenges—from understanding introversion to excelling in leadership. The insightful exploration of introvert leadership in this book challenges the conventional perception of what it means to be a leader. The steps outlined for introverts to lead effectively are a revelation, proving that leadership is not about being the loudest in the room but about leveraging one's innate strengths to inspire and influence. I wish Rohit good luck with this book and happy reading to all!!!"

– Rajat Raheja
Division President, Amdocs India;
Chair, NASSCOM GCC Pune Chapter

Making an Impact in a Noisy World:

"Rohit's INTROVATIVE brilliantly addresses the often-overlooked strengths that introverts bring to an organization. Through detailed strategies and real-world examples, this book teaches introverts how to leverage their deep thinking and reflective qualities to make impactful contributions in any role. An invaluable resource for anyone who has ever felt undervalued in a noisy world. This book equips introverts with the tools to excel and lead in any organizational role."

– Thota Nagadhar
CPTO - Xpressbees,
Founder - TekIQ Software Solutions, USA

Navigating from Introvert to INTROVATIVE:

"After helping us explore our individual Goldilocks zones, Rohit Chowdhry takes on a vital and relevant subject: The world of introverts and how they can navigate their professional corporate lives. Making the journey from Introversion to Introvation is also a way of negotiating personal spaces and Rohit brings this alive with personal stories, interactive exercises, and quizzes. This book is a must for all introverts but equally relevant to understanding how to deal with introverts, be more sensitized to their needs if you are not one and help bring out the best in them. Congratulations, Rohit, on another winner!"

– Geeta Rao
Writer, Influencer, former Creative Director Ogilvy, India

Fostering Workplace Inclusivity:

"INTROVATIVE deeply resonates with the values of inclusivity and empowerment in the workplace. Rohit masterfully outlines strategies and provides practical advice, coupled with interactive exercises, offering people associated with introversion a clear path to leverage their strengths, excel in corporate environments, and advance their careers. This book's distinctiveness lies in its dual focus on personal development and systemic change. As a senior Talent leader, I see immense value in INTROVATIVE for Human Resources professionals and business leaders alike. This must-read book fosters an understanding of introversion, paving the way for a more inclusive and dynamic workforce. Kudos to Rohit for this invaluable contribution."

– Ramakrishna Momidi
Senior HR Leader, MNC;
Vice President, National HRD Network, Hyderabad Chapter

Strategies for Career and Personal Growth:

"With INTROVATIVE, Rohit has crafted an essential manual for introverts navigating the complex dynamics of modern workplaces. This book is a thorough exploration of the introvert's journey through professional environments, providing both survival strategies and a customized blueprint for success in alignment with their inherent nature. Rohit's approach helps introverts harness their unique qualities to foster career advancement and personal growth. Insightful and practical, Rohit offers a lifeline for introverts aiming to climb the corporate ladder on their own terms."

– Gurmit Singh
General Manager, APAC & MEA at Quora
(Former CEO of Forbes India,
Former Managing Director of Yahoo India)

Strategic Steps for Introvert Success:

"Rohit's book is a ground-breaking guide for introverts seeking to excel in the corporate world. Drawing from his extensive coaching experience and interactions with professionals, the book provides introverts with seven key steps to leave their mark effectively. As someone committed to pioneering innovation globally, I see this as a transformative resource for anyone looking to drive change from within. A stellar read for enhancing one's career through introspective leadership, transcending conventional personality typing methods like MBTI."

– Dr. Sunil Gupta
Lifetime Master Trainer, Edward de Bono,
CEO – Ideas Management Consultants, Dubai

Inciting Paradigm Shifts:

"A must-read for introverts aiming to leverage their strengths for leadership success. Rohit offers actionable strategies to help introverts surmount common challenges and misconceptions. He facilitates introspection, highlighting the diverse and misunderstood strengths of introversion. Readers are left feeling more self-assured in their ability to lead authentically and create a positive impact in their personal and professional spheres."

– Sabrina Williams
MPS, I-O Psychology Practitioner,
Washington, D.C., U.S.A.

(Sabrina Williams specializes in personal and professional development, empowering individuals to realize their capabilities. She advocates for marginalized individuals and assists them in building a positive self-image by offering essential tools and resources.)

* * * * *

This book is dedicated to all the introverts who dare to defy convention, embrace their authenticity, and thrive in the corporate world with steadfast determination and unwavering resolve.

May this book serve as a guiding light on your journey to success.

Contents

Foreword by
Mr. Jayesh Ranjan, IAS

Special Chief Secretary
Information Technology,
Electronics & Communications (ITE&C) and
Industries & Commerce (I&C) Departments
Government of Telangana

Dear Readers,

It is with great pleasure that I write this foreword for "INTROVATIVE," a book dedicated to unlocking the potential of introverts in the workplace.

Having spent over three decades in public service, overseeing policies, fostering innovation, and driving development initiatives, I have witnessed first-hand how diverse perspectives and individual strengths significantly expedite progress. Introverts, with their profound analytical skills, creativity, and thoughtful approach, possess a unique advantage in navigating complex challenges and generating impactful solutions.

To accelerate results in public service and corporate settings alike, it is crucial for introverts to leverage their innate abilities. This involves fostering a workplace culture that values introspection, prioritizes collaboration over competition, and encourages deep, focused work. By harnessing these qualities, introverts can drive efficiency and innovation, ultimately leading to swifter advancements in governance and industry.

Moreover, introverts can enhance their effectiveness by embracing strategic networking and effective communication tailored to their personality traits. Rather than conforming to extroverted norms, introverts can cultivate meaningful connections and influence outcomes through thoughtful engagement and well-articulated ideas. This approach not only amplifies their impact but also fosters a more inclusive and dynamic organizational environment.

As demonstrated in my initiatives promoting digital transformation and sustainable development, introverts can excel by focusing on substantive contributions, strategic planning, and collaborative leadership. By recognizing and harnessing these inherent strengths, introverts can play a pivotal role in driving progressive change and achieving accelerated results in their respective fields.

"INTROVATIVE," authored by Rohit R. Chowdhry, provides practical insights and strategies tailored for introverts seeking to thrive in today's competitive corporate landscape. This book is not just a guide but a catalyst for inclusivity, promoting a workplace culture that embraces introversion and enhances overall well-being for both employees and organizations.

I commend Rohit for addressing this crucial topic and providing a roadmap for introverts to succeed and innovate in their professional journeys. "INTROVATIVE" is a testament to the fact that true innovation and progress are achieved when we embrace and celebrate our differences.

– Jayesh Ranjan, IAS

Acknowledgments

I am deeply grateful to the innumerable individuals who have contributed to the creation of this book, whether through their direct involvement, inspiration, or support.

First and foremost, I extend my heartfelt thanks to my family, whose unwavering encouragement and understanding made this endeavor possible. Their patience and belief in me sustained me through the highs and lows of the writing process.

To my friends, colleagues, clients, and stakeholders, your insights and perspectives enriched the content of this book immeasurably. Your willingness to share your experiences and expertise shaped the narrative and broadened its scope.

I extend my sincere appreciation to all those who provided their valuable input and offered advance praise for the book. Your feedback was instrumental in shaping its final form.

A special mention goes to my teachers, mentors, and coaches, whose guidance and wisdom have been invaluable throughout my journey as an author. Your encouragement pushed me to surpass my own expectations and delve deeper into the subject matter.

I am deeply thankful to my parents for their upbringing and values that have profoundly shaped me. Though they are no longer with us, their love and guidance continue to inspire me every day.

I am indebted to Geeta Rao, Santosh GL, Sid Priyadarshi, Vandana Waghray, Rajeev Chowdhry, and Aasheesh Chowdhry for their invaluable ideas and suggestions, which helped refine the concepts explored in this book.

A special thanks to my wife, Preeti, whose steadfast support, and belief in me never wavered, even during the most challenging moments of this journey.

Last but not least, I extend my gratitude to the team at Publishers Notion Press for their unwavering support and dedication in bringing this book to life. Their professionalism and expertise were invaluable throughout the publishing process.

To everyone who played a part in bringing this book to fruition, I offer my sincerest thanks. Your contributions have left an indelible mark on its pages, and for that, I am profoundly grateful.

Transformational Journeys – The Tale of Three Introverts

Chapter 1

Introverts in Their Own Right

Prologue: The Unspoken Power of Introverts

In a world that often celebrates the outspoken and the overtly confident, the nuanced strengths of introversion remain largely unspoken. Yet, within the contemplative minds and introspective souls of introverts, we find untapped depths of creativity, insight, and resilience.

This section of the book embarks on a journey into the lives of Ravi, Pooja, and Vivek—three introverts navigating the dynamic corporate landscape of Hyderabad. Their experiences, marked by challenges and triumphs, reveal that being reserved is not a hurdle to overcome but a profound trait to be harnessed.

Their stories reflect the broader narrative of introverts in the workplace, illustrating how introverts' introspective and thoughtful nature can be a formidable force in a world seemingly designed for extroverts. Through their journeys, we delve into the myriad ways in which silence can indeed speak volumes, and reflection can be as potent as action.

As we turn the pages of their lives, I invite you to explore the world of introverts—a world rich with internal dialogue, where quiet moments of contemplation fuel inner growth and creativity. Welcome to a journey of inner transformation, a voyage to uncover and celebrate the hidden strength of introverts.

Join me in discovering how the power of introverted individuals like Ravi, Pooja, and Vivek not only navigates but also thrives in the bustling corporate arenas. Their paths illuminate introverts' valuable contributions, challenging societal preconceptions and highlighting the need for a more inclusive understanding of success and leadership.

This prologue sets the stage for a deeper exploration of introversion in the workplace, paving the way for the following chapters, each dedicated to unraveling the complexities, challenges, and opportunities that lie in embracing one's introverted nature in an extroverted world.

So, as we embark on this enlightening journey together, let us uncover the myriad ways in which introverts, often misunderstood, hold within them the power to inspire, innovate, and lead with a quiet confidence that resonates far beyond the confines of the spoken word.

Welcome to the unspoken power of introverts.

The Unseen Strength

Metavistar Solutions, nestled among the vibrant tech parks of Hyderabad, was a hive of activity and innovation. The company's open-plan office buzzed with the chatter of collaboration and the clinks of coffee cups, a testament to its dynamic work culture. Yet, within this bustling environment, Ravi, Pooja, and Vivek navigated their daily tasks quietly, their contributions often overshadowed by the more vocally assertive members of their teams.

Ravi's Challenge

Ravi, a software engineer with a knack for solving complex coding puzzles, sat in a corner of the workspace, headphones on, deeply engrossed in his latest project. Despite his brilliant solutions, he struggled to make his voice heard in team meetings.

During one such meeting, Ravi tentatively raised a hand, "I've been thinking about a more efficient algorithm for our project that could potentially save us a lot of processing time."

A colleague interjected before he could further explain, "That sounds good, but let's stick to the plan for now. We can't afford to experiment with deadlines looming."

Ravi's suggestion was dismissed before it could even be properly considered. He retreated into his shell; his idea left unexplored.

Pooja's Silent Creativity

Pooja, the marketing strategist known for her meticulous campaigns, found solace in the quiet of early mornings before the office filled up. Her strategies were innovative, but she shied away from the spotlight, preferring to let her work speak for itself.

"Pooja, your campaign ideas are excellent, but we need you to be more vocal. Share your thoughts in our brainstorming sessions," her manager suggested during a one-to-one meeting.

"I understand, but it's hard for me to think in loud environments," Pooja admitted, feeling the weight of expectations to conform to a more extroverted communication style.

Vivek's Networking Hurdles

Vivek, with his keen eye for financial detail, often found himself at odds with the company's emphasis on networking. The after-work gatherings, a whirlwind of small talk and laughter, felt like an alien world to him.

At one such event, Vivek stood awkwardly with a drink in hand, trying to fit in. A colleague approached, chatting about the latest office gossip. Vivek managed a polite smile, his mind elsewhere, pondering over the budget report he had left on his desk.

"I just don't get how casual conversations at these events can lead to professional opportunities," Vivek later confided to a close colleague.

Anjali's Arrival

The turning point for Ravi, Pooja, and Vivek came with the arrival of Anjali, a senior VP known for her innovative leadership style. Anjali had a different vision for the team, one that recognized the quiet strength of its introverted members.

Anjali organized a "Harnessing Your Inner Strength" workshop, inviting Ravi, Pooja, Vivek, and others who felt overlooked. The conference room, usually a place of daunting presentations and heated discussions, was transformed into a haven of introspection and discovery that day.

"Welcome, everyone. Today, we're not here to talk about what you should do better according to the usual standards. Instead, we'll explore how your unique qualities can be your greatest assets," Anjali began, her voice calm yet commanding attention.

Ravi listened intently as Anjali spoke about the power of listening and reflection, thinking about the algorithm he hadn't dared to advocate for strongly.

Pooja felt a surge of hope when Anjali mentioned the importance of creativity and behind-the-scenes strategizing, realizing her quiet approach had its strengths.

Vivek nodded along as Anjali discussed one-to-one networking and deep, meaningful connections rather than superficial socializing.

"As introverts, your power lies in your depth of thought, your ability to listen, and your creative solutions. It's about leveraging these strengths in a way that suits you," Anjali concluded, her eyes sweeping across the room, meeting those of Ravi, Pooja, and Vivek.

Their transformation journey had just begun, sparked by Anjali's belief in the unspoken power of introverts. As the workshop ended, the trio lingered, a sense of camaraderie forming among them. They shared their experiences and challenges, but more importantly, they shared a newfound hope and determination to harness their introversion as a strength.

Ravi felt inspired to propose his algorithm again, this time in a detailed email to his team. Pooja decided to create a visual presentation of her next campaign, letting her creativity shine through in a way that felt natural to her. Vivek began to see the value in smaller, more intimate professional gatherings where genuine connections could be made.

Metavistar Solutions was on the brink of a cultural shift that would not only embrace the loud and the assertive but also recognize the quiet power lying dormant within its introverted innovators.

Chapter 2

Confronting the Situation

In the weeks following Anjali's transformative workshop, Ravi, Pooja, and Vivek embarked on a journey of self-discovery and adaptation, each finding their unique way to navigate the extroverted world of Metavistar Solutions.

Ravi's Written Voice

Ravi sat at his desk, staring at the computer screen, drafting an email to his team. This time, he was determined to ensure his idea wouldn't just be another voice drowned out in a meeting. He carefully outlined his proposed algorithm, explaining its efficiency and potential impact on the project's timeline.

> Subject: Innovative Solution Proposal - Streamlining Project X's Processing Time
>
> Dear Team,
>
> I hope this message finds you well. I've been exploring potential enhancements for our current project and have developed an algorithm that could significantly improve our processing efficiency. Attached, you'll find a detailed overview, including simulations and expected outcomes.

I believe this could be a game-changer for us and would love to discuss it further at your convenience.

Best, Ravi

To Ravi's surprise, the response was overwhelmingly positive. His manager quickly scheduled a meeting to discuss the proposal in detail. For the first time, Ravi felt his ideas were truly being heard and valued.

Pooja's Creative Haven

Pooja had always found solace in the early morning hours, the office quiet and still. It was during these moments that she felt her creativity flow most freely. Inspired by Anjali's workshop, she decided to transform her workspace into a reflection of her inner world, a place where her ideas could flourish.

She introduced plants, whose greenery brought a sense of calm and renewal. Noise-canceling headphones allowed her to immerse herself in the worlds she created through her marketing campaigns, undisturbed by the office buzz.

Pooja's next campaign presentation was unlike any before. She used a narrative approach, weaving a story that not only outlined the strategy but also captured the brand's essence in a way that resonated with everyone in the room.

"As you can see," Pooja concluded, her voice steady, "our campaign invites the audience into a story where they are not just consumers but participants in a journey. Each visual and word is a step further into the world we are creating for them."

The room erupted in applause, her team's excitement palpable. Pooja's approach captivated her audience and set a new standard for creativity and engagement in the department.

Vivek's Genuine Connections

Vivek had always felt out of place at the large, noisy networking events that seemed to define professional growth at Metavistar Solutions. Taking Anjali's advice to heart, he began seeking out smaller, more intimate settings where genuine conversations could occur.

He reached out to colleagues for one-to-one coffee meetings, focusing on topics beyond mere work - discussing interests, goals, and vision for the future. These interactions, though initially out of his comfort zone, soon revealed a network of connections based on mutual respect and shared aspirations.

One such meeting with a colleague from the product development team led to an unexpected collaboration. They discovered a mutual interest in sustainable business practices, sparking a series of discussions on how their departments could work together to incorporate these values into Metavistar's projects.

"I've always believed that our company could lead the way in sustainability," Vivek shared, enthusiasm evident in his voice.

"And with your financial expertise and our team's innovations, I think we can make a real impact," his colleague replied, equally inspired.

A Turning Point

The mid-year review marked a significant turning point for Ravi, Pooja, and Vivek. Their manager praised their contributions, noting the unique ways they had each stepped forward. Ravi's algorithm had streamlined project workflows, Pooja's campaigns had seen unprecedented engagement, and Vivek's cross-departmental collaborations were paving the way for innovative practices at Metavistar.

Encouraged by their success, Anjali proposed an idea: a series of workshops led by Ravi, Pooja, and Vivek titled "Introvert Innovators." The workshops would share their journey and strategies, offering support and inspiration to others who might feel overshadowed in the extroverted corporate world.

As they prepared for their first workshop, the trio reflected on their journey. They had not only found a way to navigate their workplace dynamics but had also become mentors, ready to guide others in finding strength in their introversion.

Their efforts were transforming Metavistar Solutions, creating a culture where the quiet strength of introverts was recognized as a powerful asset, forever changing the way the company approached innovation, creativity, and leadership.

Chapter 3

The Crucial Test

The "AvsAR" project was Metavistar Solutions' ambitious venture into augmented reality, a flagship project that demanded not just technical prowess but innovative thinking and cohesive team leadership. Ravi, Pooja, and Vivek found themselves at the heart of this pivotal project, each facing unique challenges that would test their newfound confidence and strategies.

Ravi's Leadership

Ravi was appointed to lead the coding team, a role that required not just technical expertise but the ability to guide and inspire his team. He approached this challenge with a blend of written directives for clarity and inclusivity in meetings to ensure every voice was heard.

In one of the initial team meetings, Ravi introduced the project outline, carefully detailing each segment through a shared document he had prepared. "I've outlined our primary objectives and the technical challenges we might face," Ravi explained, projecting the document on the screen. "I want to hear your thoughts, especially any concerns or alternative approaches you might have."

Shefali, a reserved team member, began to share her views. Just as she started, Kartik, the outspoken extrovert, interjected with fervor, stealing the spotlight. Ravi intervened, taking a deep breath, and raising his hand to catch the group's attention. "Please let Shefali complete," he asserted calmly, his voice cutting through the room. Kartik paused, surprised by Ravi's interruption. "Of course, please go ahead," he conceded, gesturing for Shefali to proceed. After the meeting, Shefali caught up with Ravi, thanked him, and assured him that she would follow his example the next time she or someone else faced a similar situation.

The team responded well to Ravi's methodical and open approach, feeling valued and motivated. Under his leadership, they navigated the project's complexities with a sense of unity and purpose.

Pooja's Innovative Campaign

Pooja's task was to develop a marketing campaign that would not only launch "AvsAR" but also capture the imagination of the industry and consumers alike. She delved into market research, merging data-driven insights with creative visuals to craft a campaign narrative that was both compelling and innovative.

During a brainstorming session with her team, Pooja shared a mock-up of the campaign's centerpiece, a visual story that illustrated the impact of "AvsAR" on everyday life. "Imagine stepping into a world where the boundaries between reality and digital are seamlessly blended. That's the journey we want to take our audience on," Pooja articulated, her passion for the project shining through.

The campaign set new standards for creativity and engagement, generating buzz and anticipation long before the product's launch.

Vivek's Financial Acumen

Vivek faced the challenge of managing "AvsAR's" budget, ensuring the project remained financially viable without stifling innovation.

His strategic planning and negotiation skills were put to the test as he worked to secure resources at optimal costs.

In a pivotal negotiation with a key software vendor, Vivek found himself facing unexpected resistance. The vendor, aware of the project's potential, was adamant about the premium price of their technology.

Undeterred, Vivek leaned forward, his eyes locking with the vendor's. "We're on the brink of something ground-breaking with AvsAR," he began, his voice unwavering despite the tension in the room. "But for us to proceed, the cost must align with our budgetary constraints."

A palpable silence filled the air as Vivek's words hung between them, the weight of the decision resting heavily on both parties. After what felt like an eternity, the vendor relented, recognizing Vivek's unwavering commitment to the project's success. With a firm handshake, they reached a mutually beneficial agreement, ensuring that "AvsAR" could continue its journey toward innovation without compromising its financial stability.

Vivek's ability to form personal connections and his strategic mindset led to successful negotiations, keeping the project on track without compromising its innovative edge.

Collaborative Problem-Solving

Midway through the development, the team encountered a significant hurdle: a key component of the software was not integrating as planned, risking the project's timeline and viability. Ravi convened an emergency meeting, calling on Pooja and Vivek for their input.

"We need to find a solution that keeps us within budget but also meets our launch timeline," Ravi stated, opening the floor for discussion.

Pooja suggested leveraging the issue as a storytelling opportunity for the marketing campaign, turning the challenge into a narrative of innovation and determination. "It's about how we overcome obstacles, not just the obstacles themselves. Let's share this journey with our audience," she proposed.

Vivek, meanwhile, worked out a revised financial plan that allowed for additional resources to address the integration issue without derailing the budget. "If we re-allocate funds from less critical areas and negotiate some additional support from our vendors, we can make this work," Vivek outlined, his expertise shining through.

Together, the trio developed a comprehensive strategy that addressed the technical challenge while maintaining the project's momentum. Their collaborative problem-solving not only saved "AvsAR" but also demonstrated the effectiveness of their quiet leadership.

Their success in leading the project to its triumphant launch shattered stereotypes within Metavistar Solutions and the industry at large. Ravi, Pooja, and Vivek had proven that introverted qualities—deep thinking, focused listening, and calm assertiveness—were not just valuable but indispensable in leadership roles. The "AvsAR" project became a testament to the strength that lies in quiet confidence, changing perceptions and setting a new precedent for what leadership looks like.

Chapter 4

The Victory Within

The successful launch of "AvsAR" was a defining moment for Metavistar Solutions and a personal victory for Ravi, Pooja, and Vivek. Their contributions had been pivotal to the project's success, marking a significant milestone in their careers and their personal growth.

Ravi: The Reflective Leader

Ravi's office bore the marks of his new role as Lead Software Engineer. Certificates of recognition and photos of his team adorned the walls, a testament to their achievements. Yet, it was the reflective confidence with which he now approached his duties that truly signified his transformation.

In a team meeting, Ravi shared his vision for the next project, his voice steady and assured. "The 'AvsAR' project taught us the value of collaboration and innovative thinking. Let's carry those lessons forward, pushing the boundaries of what we can achieve together."

After the meeting, a junior engineer approached him, expressing admiration for Ravi's leadership style. "I've always been more reserved, and seeing you lead has inspired me. I now realize that my introversion can be a strength, not a barrier."

Ravi smiled, realizing the impact he had not only on the projects but also on his colleagues, fostering an environment where reflective confidence could thrive.

Pooja: The Creative Force

Pooja's workspace was an oasis of creativity, with sketches and storyboards highlighting the narrative depth of her campaigns. The success of 'AvsAR' not only showcased her innovative approach but also established her as a beacon for aspiring marketers.

As Pooja stood before the company's leadership, the anticipation in the room was palpable. Her latest campaign concept promised to be a game-changer, and everyone leaned in eagerly as she began to unveil her vision.

Just as she reached the climax of her presentation, the lights flickered and then abruptly went out. Gasps filled the room as darkness enveloped them. Undeterred, Pooja took a deep breath and continued to narrate her campaign concept, her voice steady and unwavering despite the unexpected interruption. "Our campaigns are more than just advertisements; they're invitations to experience the world through our products," she explained, her words reflecting her passion for storytelling. With nothing but the glow of emergency lights illuminating her sketches, she painted a vivid picture that left her audience spellbound.

When the lights finally returned, Pooja concluded her presentation to a thunderous applause. Her ability to maintain composure and deliver a compelling narrative even in the face of adversity showcased not just her creativity but her unwavering determination to inspire others through her work. Later, a colleague commented, "Your work on 'AvsAR' has been a game-changer for us. It's not just the creativity; it's the way you see the world that inspires us all."

Pooja's influence had extended beyond her campaigns, inspiring her team to explore their own creativity and bring a deeper level of engagement to their work.

Vivek: The Strategic Connector

Vivek's office was a hub of activity, with financial models and strategic plans spread across his desk. His role had expanded beyond budgeting to shaping the strategic direction of Metavistar's future projects, thanks to his innovative financial strategies and ability to forge meaningful connections.

In a strategy session, Vivek outlined a new approach to project financing, one that maximized innovation while maintaining fiscal responsibility. "By leveraging our networks and building partnerships, we can unlock new funding avenues, reducing our reliance on traditional budgeting methods," he proposed, his colleagues nodding in agreement.

As the meeting concluded, one of the senior managers approached him, saying, "Your work has not only ensured the viability of our projects but has also opened new pathways for growth. Your ability to connect on a deeper level, to think beyond numbers, is what sets you apart."

Vivek's success redefined the role of finance within the company, highlighting the importance of strategic thinking and genuine relationships in driving the company's growth.

A Cultural Shift

As Ravi, Pooja, and Vivek gathered in the cafeteria, reflecting on their journey, they realized the profound impact they had made. They had not only achieved personal success but had also inspired a cultural shift within Metavistar Solutions.

"We've shown that leadership isn't about being the loudest in the room," Ravi mused. "It's about having the vision and the confidence to guide others, regardless of where you fall on the introvert-extrovert spectrum."

Pooja added, "And creativity isn't just about bright colors and loud campaigns. It's about connecting with people on a deeper level, telling stories that resonate."

Vivek nodded, "It's also about showing that finance isn't just about numbers. It's about understanding the bigger picture, the deeper connections that drive our company forward."

Their dialogue stood as a clear marker of their evolution, not solely in their careers but as people who had fully embraced their introverted selves to lead and motivate others. They had laid the groundwork for the next generation of leadership at Metavistar Solutions, demonstrating how the subtle power of introversion can indeed be a formidable influence on the future.

Against the backdrop of Hyderabad's evening skyline, bathed in a golden light that enveloped the Metavistar Solutions campus, Ravi, Pooja, and Vivek stood side by side, pondering over their shared journey. Beginning as individuals who once felt overshadowed in an environment that appeared to celebrate the extroverted, they had risen to become beacons of leadership, innovation, and mentorship. Their narrative had transformed into a source of inspiration and a validation of the profound power found in serene reflection, thoughtful analysis, and the bravery in owning one's introversion.

A Message of Hope

In a brightly lit conference room filled with eager faces from various departments, the trio prepared to share their journey through the "Introvert Innovators" workshop series. The room buzzed with anticipation, a palpable sense of curiosity and excitement filling the space.

"Welcome, everyone," Ravi began, his voice steady and confident. "Today, we're here to share a different narrative about success in the corporate world. A narrative that celebrates the power of introversion."

Pooja took over, her presence calm yet commanding. "We'll share our personal stories, the challenges we faced, and how we turned what many consider a 'weakness' into our greatest strength."

Vivek concluded the introduction, his tone sincere. "Our journey is a testament to the fact that success isn't about conforming to a standard mold. It's about understanding and leveraging your unique traits, even in environments that don't seem to accommodate them at first glance."

The Workshop Series

As the workshop unfolded, Ravi, Pooja, and Vivek shared insights into their strategies for overcoming obstacles and making their voices heard. They spoke of the importance of finding one's preferred mode of communication, creating environments that foster creativity, and building meaningful connections based on genuine understanding rather than superficial networking.

Participants were encouraged to engage in group discussions, sharing their experiences and aspirations. The atmosphere was one of mutual support and recognition, a space where introverts could see their reflections in the stories of the speakers and feel validated in their struggles and strengths.

Impact and Reflection

After the workshop, a young analyst approached the trio, her eyes bright with newfound determination. "I've always felt out of place with my reserved nature, but hearing your stories today has given me hope. I see now that my introversion is not a barrier but a unique lens through which I view the world. Thank you for sharing your journey."

Ravi smiled, recalling his own doubts and how far he had come. "Remember, your introversion is a strength. Embrace it, and you'll find ways to shine on your terms."

Pooja added, "Creativity and innovation aren't loud. They come from a place of deep reflection. Your quiet space is where your best ideas will flourish."

"And never underestimate the value of genuine connections," Vivek chimed in. "They can be your strongest allies in navigating the corporate landscape."

As the evening drew to a close, the trio stood together once more, looking out at the city lights. Their journey had not only transformed their own lives but had begun to shift the culture within Metavistar Solutions, making it a place where introverts and extroverts alike could thrive.

A Legacy of Change

Their "Introvert Innovators" workshop sparked a movement within the company, leading to more inclusive policies and practices that recognized and valued the diverse strengths of all employees. Ravi, Pooja, and Vivek had not only carved a path for themselves but had paved the way for future generations of introverts in the corporate world.

Their story was a powerful message of hope and action, a reminder that embracing one's inner power, regardless of how the world perceives it, can lead to unimaginable success and fulfillment. They showed that in the spectrum of human traits, every strand, no matter how faint or silent, contributes to the collective vibrancy.

As the narrative of Ravi, Pooja, and Vivek concludes, their legacy continues to inspire, encouraging introverts everywhere to embrace their power within, to shine in their unique light, and to redefine the landscape of leadership and innovation in the corporate world and beyond.

Chapter 5

Reflections and Introduction to Further Exploration

Epilogue:

Dear Reader,

As we turn the final page on the journey of Ravi, Pooja, and Vivek, we pause to reflect on the profound narrative they've left in their wake—a narrative that echoes the silent yet powerful odyssey of countless introverts navigating the vibrant but often challenging corporate landscape. Their story is more than an account of personal triumph; it is a guide, a ray of hope for those who tread the path less vocalized yet rich with the potential for unparalleled innovation and leadership.

Key Takeaways: A Prelude to Action

1. **Value Your Introverted Nature:** Recognize that introversion offers a unique perspective in a world that thrives on diversity of thought. Your capacity for reflection and deep thinking is a formidable asset in understanding complex issues and crafting thoughtful solutions.

2. **Find Your Unique Voice:** Communication transcends volume. Discover and hone a style that reflects your insights and perspectives, much like Ravi's adeptness with written expression, ensuring your ideas are acknowledged and valued.

3. **Create Your Space:** Design environments that nurture your creativity and focus, like Pooja's sanctuary of innovation. These spaces, physical or temporal, are essential for your productivity and well-being.

4. **Build Meaningful Connections:** Emulate Vivek's approach to forming genuine relationships rather than superficial networks. Depth trumps breadth in building alliances that are both rewarding and sustainable.

5. **Embrace Your Strengths in Leadership:** Leverage your innate abilities to listen and empathize, fostering a team dynamic that is cohesive, motivated, and inspired by a shared vision.

6. **Seek out Allies:** Surround yourself with mentors and peers who recognize and celebrate the value of your introverted qualities. Together, navigate the challenges and opportunities of the corporate world with mutual support and understanding.

A Message of Encouragement:

To the introverts in the workforce, know this: your qualities are indispensable. In a corporate world that often prizes the immediate and the outspoken, there lies untapped power in the quiet depths of introspection and the richness of thoughtful action. Embrace your introverted nature as Ravi, Pooja, and Vivek did, for it is the wellspring of your unique strengths and the foundation of your success.

Your journey, though it may be marked by moments of silence, is profound. It is a testament to the fact that the measure of success is not the volume of one's voice but the impact of one's contributions—the authenticity of your words, the innovation of your ideas, and the depth of your insights.

Toward a Future Illuminated by Introversion:

As we bid farewell to the narrative of our three guides, let this not be the end but a beginning—a prologue to your journey of self-discovery and professional achievement. The section that follows, from understanding the essence of introversion to mastering the art of leadership and collaboration, is designed to equip you with the strategies and insights to navigate the workplace as an introvert.

- **Chapters on Understanding Introversion, Overcoming Challenges, and Embracing Your Strengths** lay the foundation for recognizing and leveraging your innate abilities.
- **Strategies for Effective Communication, Networking, and Teamwork** provide practical **steps** to enhance your professional interactions and collaborations.
- **Guidance on Introvert Leadership and Sustaining Success** offers a roadmap to achieving and maintaining a position of influence and fulfillment in your career.

Each chapter is a step on the path to amplifying your introverted strengths, designed to inspire action, foster growth, and celebrate the quiet power that propels you toward success.

As you embark on this journey, remember: the world needs your insight, your vision, and your voice. Embrace your introversion, foster your unique capabilities, and let your quiet strength shine brightly.

Sincerely,

Rohit R Chowdhry

SECTION 2

Insights

Breaking my own Boundaries: Embracing Discomfort to forge my Path.

As a young dreamer of ten, I aspired to soar the skies as an Air Force pilot, enrolling in a prestigious institution dedicated to molding future defense officers. Despite my fervent aspirations, the rejection from the forces redirected me toward civilian life, where I charted a new course in commerce, aiming to become a Chartered Accountant. Although this departure from my childhood dreams was significant, I approached it with unwavering resolve, unaware of the twist of fate awaiting me.

During the anticipation of my B. Com exam results, I ventured into the world of technology by enrolling in a part-time computer course in 1990, when computers were still shrouded in mystery. Eager to unravel the secrets of this evolving landscape, I took my first steps into this uncharted territory.

While immersed in the complexities of computer training, a notice for summer trainees in marketing caught my eye, offering a chance to break free from my comfort zone. Seizing the opportunity with some anxiety and excitement, I plunged into the realm of software application business development, meeting new people each day, confronting new challenges, and honing my persuasive skills.

Navigating the intricate paths of commerce and technology against the backdrop of bustling offices and streets, I discovered a passion for building connections and aligning efforts toward organizational goals in the corporate landscape. Leveraging my introverted strengths, I carved a niche for myself in the dynamic world of IT, transitioning from sales and marketing roles to profit center management and leadership positions in offshore operations.

Reflecting on the winding path that led me here, I realize that success often lies beyond comfort zones. Embracing the unknown, I uncovered the essence of introverted strength, finding fulfillment in the pursuit of my dreams. My ability to connect and build relationships played a pivotal role in navigating my journey, offering unwavering support and guidance in moments of uncertainty.

Moreover, I discovered the power of strategic behaviors and tactical maneuvers, from pursuing the art of public speaking, presentations, and networking to cultivating quiet confidence. These tactics served as a compass guiding me through my career path.

Amidst the hustle and bustle of corporate life, it was the human connection that remained the cornerstone of my journey, fueling my passion and propelling me forward. Alongside this, my interest in supporting the development of people grew, as I realized the profound impact of mentorship and collaboration on personal and professional growth.

As I stand on these new horizons, armed with invaluable lessons learned, I embark on the next chapter of my adventure, believing in the threads of connection that weave the fabric of our destiny. At this stage of my journey, I find it to be my solemn objective in penning down this book: to extend a helping hand to my fellow introverts. Through sharing my experiences and the lessons learned along the way, it is my earnest desire to offer support and guidance, enabling others to navigate their own paths with confidence and resilience. Together, let us embrace our introverted strengths and forge ahead on the journey toward fulfillment and success.

Chapter 1

Is This Book for You?

This book is a culmination of the strategies I employed, the experiences of those I've had the privilege to coach, and the barriers we collectively overcame. It's crafted as a guide to expedite your success in the workplace as an introvert, drawing from a wealth of shared experiences and challenges.

Let me take you on my journey from taking a leap of faith into the corporate world, driven by a conscious decision to step outside my comfort zone, to where I stand today. My initial foray into sales was marked by the gradual and often challenging process of building credibility, a path that seems to stretch a bit longer and feels more arduous for us introverts. Despite the challenges, I was fortunate to cross paths with leaders, managers, and colleagues who, consciously and sometimes unconsciously, supported and nurtured my introverted nature.

Embarking on this journey often felt like swimming against a powerful current, battling the overwhelming energy of an extrovert-dominated environment at every pitch and meeting. The encouragement and understanding I received along the way were invaluable, offering me solace and motivation to persevere.

Choosing not to surrender to the daunting challenges, I committed myself to push beyond my comfort zone. This decision was not without its moments of doubt and introspection, where the prospect of success seemed distant. Yet, I persisted, driven by the belief in the value of perseverance. Throughout this journey, I've acquired insights into how introverts can not only survive but truly thrive in the dynamic world of business.

Welcome to the first chapter of our journey together! This chapter is designed to introduce who this book is for and its potential benefits for you—whether you're an introvert navigating your career aspirations or someone aiming to understand introverts in the workplace better. I will delve into the purpose of this book and highlight a few key points about my writing style, setting the stage for what to expect in the chapters that follow.

Who Is This Book For?

If you've ever encountered feedback like "You need to speak up more, be more vocal in meetings, you should network more, put yourself out there," or "You come across as too reserved or shy, it might hold you back from leadership opportunities," and if this sounds all too familiar, you are not alone. This book is specifically tailored for introverts who face such challenges in professional settings. Embark on a self-assessment in the next chapter to see if you resonate with introverted traits—this book is written with you in mind.

Why Is This Book Helpful to You?

There exists a prevalent misconception that introversion acts as a barrier to professional advancement. The true obstacle is not introversion itself but rather the misconceived notion that it impedes progress. This book aims to transform perspectives, equipping introverts with strategies to propel their careers forward, understanding that introverts might unintentionally signal a lack of ambition through their quiet demeanor, affecting their growth and success prospects. Here, you'll find insights into navigating these and other challenges, forging a path to advancement that aligns with your introverted nature.

Your Career Aspiration

In the pursuit of career aspirations, it's crucial to recognize that different roles demand different personality styles. For instance, positions requiring frequent networking, dynamic communication, and swift decision-making often favor individuals with outgoing personalities. However, it's equally important to acknowledge the potential pitfalls of consistently pushing oneself outside of their comfort zone. While occasional adaptability is commendable, sustained efforts to do so can lead to stress and burnout.

True success often stems from aligning oneself with roles and environments that complement one's natural personality style. Every personality type harbors unique strengths and opportunities for achievement. For example, outgoing individuals often thrive in roles that involve extensive interaction, public speaking, and performance. Conversely, those with a more reserved demeanor may excel in analytical, strategic, and research-oriented positions that prioritize deep thinking and meticulous planning.

While it's true that certain industries and professions may seem tailor-made for introverted individuals—such as accounting, software development, IT specialties, or back-office roles —there's no need to confine oneself to these conventional paths. It's essential to **dare to pursue a career aligned with one's passion,** even if it means navigating a gap between one's inherent personality style and the perceived requirements of a desired field. Success lies in the ability to adapt behaviors and strategies that enhance performance while remaining true to oneself.

Despite prevailing societal biases toward extroversion, it's imperative to celebrate introversion as a valuable asset in the professional realm. By embracing one's unique qualities and dispelling the myth that success is exclusively reserved for extroverts, introverted individuals can leverage their inherent strengths to drive success at the workplace. INTROVATIVE serves as a guide in this journey, empowering individuals to achieve professional fulfillment while honoring their authentic nature.

INTROVATIVE presents a comprehensive approach designed specifically for introverts seeking to transform their career trajectories. This book masterfully **combines the inherent qualities of introversion with innovative strategies** to address and surmount the common obstacles and misconceptions that introverted professionals often encounter in the workplace. **"INTROVATIVE" is more than just a title; it's a bold statement for those prepared to harness their reflective strengths, pushing their careers ahead innovatively, with confidence and strategic insight.** With actionable insights and compelling anecdotes, readers will discover how to transform perceived limitations into powerful catalysts for career acceleration. This book acts as a vital navigational tool for introverts, plotting a journey where deep reflection meets innovation, leading to unparalleled career growth and satisfaction.

Unlocking Boundless Potential

The human mind is a remarkable entity, capable of immense feats of focus, creativity, and endurance. Contrary to popular belief, it is not inherently predisposed to tire easily. Rather, it becomes fatigued when engaged in tasks that fail to stimulate or captivate it fully. When individuals are immersed in activities that align with their interests, passions, or goals, they often find themselves in a state of flow, where time seems to slip away, and energy remains abundant. It is in these moments of deep engagement that the mind thrives, showcasing its boundless capacity for innovation and productivity. However, when faced with monotonous or unfulfilling tasks, the mind can quickly become drained, leading to feelings of exhaustion and disinterest. This phenomenon highlights the importance of pursuing activities that resonate with one's intrinsic motivations and values, as it is in these pursuits that the mind finds its true vitality and resilience.

Purpose of This Book

The driving force behind crafting this book is to empower fellow introverts to swiftly and confidently achieve their career aspirations. I've come to realize that introverts often possess distinct approaches to operating, communicating, collaborating and decision-making. Unfortunately, these unique behaviors are frequently misunderstood as hesitancy, reluctance, or lack of confidence, thereby impeding our progress, and limiting our opportunities for growth.

My premise is straightforward: by embracing a few behaviors outside of one's comfort zone while staying true to their authentic selves, introverts can accelerate their growth and success in the workplace.

The purpose of this book is twofold: to equip introverts with the knowledge, skills, and strategies needed to navigate the challenges of the modern workplace and to harness their unique strengths for lasting success. Through practical insights and actionable advice, the book aims to empower introverts to deepen their self-awareness, overcome obstacles, and thrive in both professional and personal spheres.

Objectives of the book:

- **Empower introverts** by enhancing their self-awareness, fostering self-acceptance, and building confidence.
- **Address workplace challenges**, including communication, networking, collaborating and leadership, to facilitate success for introverts.

- **Guide introverts in stepping boldly** by expanding their comfort zones and developing essential interpersonal and leadership skills.

- **Identify opportunities** for introverts in thriving careers, entrepreneurship, and business ventures, providing actionable strategies for success.

- **Foster inclusivity** by promoting a workplace culture that embraces introversion, prioritizes collaboration, and enhances overall well-being for both employees and organizations.

A few key points about my writing style in this book:

- **Direct Engagement:** I speak directly to you, assuming an introverted reader seeking guidance. However, one chapter, "Crafting a Workplace Environment Conducive to Introverts," speaks to a broader audience interested in nurturing an inclusive environment.

- **Personal Reflections:** Sharing personal experiences and anecdotes, I aim to connect with fellow introverts on a deeper level, hoping these stories resonate and inspire.

- **Anecdotes from my Friends:** I've also woven in personal experiences and anecdotes shared by my friends and former colleagues. To respect privacy and for creative expression, I've chosen to use fictitious names for both individuals and companies involved.

- **Interactive Elements:** Chapters include assessments and questionnaires, encouraging active participation. I recommend engaging with these tools directly within the book for a more immersive experience.

- **Actionable Content:** Chapters include practical action steps and conclude with a summary of highlights. These are crafted to distill key insights and support their implementation in real-world scenarios.

As we embark on this insightful journey together, I invite you to explore and embrace the unique strengths your introverted nature brings to the professional landscape. Let's navigate the corporate world with newfound confidence, leveraging our power within to achieve unparalleled success.

Chapter 2

Understanding Introversion

In this chapter, you will explore the intricate realm of introversion, delving into its nuances, strengths, and perceived weaknesses. Through self-assessment, embark on a journey of introspection to discern whether you align with the traits of an introvert. Unravel the unique strengths that introverts bring to the table, from keen observation skills to a deep capacity for introspection and creativity. Simultaneously, confront the misconceptions and societal biases surrounding introversion, shedding light on the perceived weaknesses that often overshadow the inherent strengths of introverted individuals. Join me as we navigate the complexities of introversion, embracing its richness and diversity in the spectrum of human personality.

Are you an Introvert?

Self-assessment

Take this self-assessment - "Am I an Introvert." Rate each of the statements on a scale of 1 to 5. Please choose the number that best represents your feelings, thoughts, and behaviors.

Less True 1   2   3   4   5 More True

S.No.	Statement	Your response
1.	I feel drained and exhausted after spending time with a large group of people.	
2.	I prefer having a few close friends rather than many acquaintances.	
3.	I feel overwhelmed when I'm the center of attention in social situations.	
4.	I often seek solitude to recharge my energy after socializing.	
5.	I find it challenging to strike up conversations with strangers.	
6.	I enjoy meaningful one-on-one conversations over group interactions.	
7.	I prefer reflecting on my thoughts and feelings alone rather than discussing them with others immediately.	
8.	I feel more comfortable expressing myself through writing rather than speaking.	
9.	I enjoy spending time alone with my hobbies and interests.	
10.	I prefer planned, intimate gatherings over spontaneous, large-scale events.	
11.	I tend to think carefully before speaking and often pause to consider my words.	
12.	I feel most at ease in quiet, calm environments.	
13.	I value deep connections and meaningful interactions over superficial socializing.	
14.	I often feel overshadowed or drowned out in group settings.	

S.No.	Statement	Your response
15.	I feel most content and rejuvenated after spending time alone.	
16.	I prefer a few close relationships with deeper connections over a wide social circle.	
17.	I enjoy solitary activities like reading, writing, or taking walks alone.	
18.	I feel anxious or uncomfortable in highly stimulating environments with lots of noise and activity.	
19.	I prefer smaller, more intimate gatherings over large parties or events.	
20.	I often need time alone to recharge and reflect on my thoughts and experiences.	

Scoring: Please add up all 'Your responses' and review your score in the Score Key.

Score Key

Score Interpretation: Here's what your score might indicate:

- Total Score 86-100: Strongly Introverted:

  You have a strong preference for solitude and introspection, finding deep fulfillment in solitary activities and meaningful one-on-one interactions. Social gatherings may be draining for you, and you often seek out quiet, peaceful environments.

- Total Score 56-85: Moderately Introverted:

  You gravitate toward more introspective pursuits and may find extended social interactions draining. Although you cherish moments spent with loved ones, you also prioritize solitary moments for introspection and rejuvenation.

- Total Score 46-55: Balanced or Ambivert:

  You exhibit a mix of introverted and extroverted tendencies, feeling comfortable in both social and solitary situations. You may adapt your behavior depending on the context and enjoy a variety of social interactions.

- Total Score 31-45: Moderately Extroverted:

  While you enjoy socializing and being around others, you also value your alone time and may occasionally need to recharge by yourself. You strike a balance between social interaction and solitary activities.

- Total Score 20-30: Strongly Extroverted:

  You likely thrive in social settings, preferring frequent interaction with others and enjoying a wide circle of acquaintances. You may find solitude draining and prefer being surrounded by people.

These descriptions offer a broad overview of an individual's placement on the introversion-extroversion spectrum, determined by their total score. It's important to recognize that each person is unique, and these scores should be viewed as guidelines rather than rigid classifications.

Signs You Might Be an Introvert

Recognizing introversion involves understanding patterns of behavior. Introverts exhibit traits such as a need for quiet concentration, reflection, self-awareness, thoughtful decision-making, comfort in solitude, preference for writing over talking, fatigue after social interactions, and deep, meaningful friendships. Taking a test, such as the Myers-Briggs Type Indicator (MBTI), can provide deeper insights into one's introverted tendencies.

Defining Introversion

Being an introvert involves both advantages and disadvantages in the realms of business and entrepreneurship. Understanding the essence of introversion is crucial for leveraging these traits effectively. Contrary to common misconceptions, introversion is not synonymous with shyness or lack of confidence. It pertains to how individuals process information and engage with their surroundings.

Introversion, as a personality trait, is marked by an inward focus and a preference for solitude or intimate settings. Introverts find comfort in moments of solitude, where they can delve into their thoughts and engage in activities conducive to contemplation. These tranquil intervals often serve as fertile ground for creativity to flourish. With their thoughtful, introspective nature, introverts thrive in environments that allow them the time and space to process information and reflect on ideas at their own pace.

Carl Jung defined introversion as a psychological orientation where an individual's energy is directed inward toward their own thoughts, feelings, and reflections. Introverts are primarily focused on their inner world and derive energy from dealing with ideas, memories, and experiences, rather than external stimuli. This orientation influences their perceptions, decision-making processes, and interactions with the external world, making them more inclined toward solitude and deep, reflective thinking.

Myers-Briggs defines introversion as a preference for focusing energy and attention inwardly toward one's own thoughts, feelings, and reflections, rather than outwardly toward people and external events. Introverted individuals are characterized by their preference for deep, solitary activities, enjoying quiet environments where they can concentrate without external interruptions. They tend to feel more energized by spending time alone or in small, intimate groups rather than large social gatherings.

Brain Chemistry Differences

Research indicates that introverts and extroverts exhibit differences in brain chemistry, specifically in dopamine, adrenaline, and acetylcholine levels. Dopamine, the "feel-good" hormone, rewards activities that stimulate its production. Extroverts, with more dopamine receptors, require higher levels to experience excitement. Introverts, being more sensitive to dopamine, may feel overwhelmed in stimulating environments.

Acetylcholine, associated with pleasure and calmness, plays a role in cognitive abilities and concentration. Introverts benefit from its effects, especially during activities like reading. Understanding these neurochemical differences provides insights into the varying characteristics and preferences of introverts.

Introversion manifests in various traits that contribute to an individual's unique approach to life, work, and relationships. In dispelling common myths, it is essential to recognize and celebrate the strengths associated with introversion.

Contrary to the myth that introverts struggle to advance in the workplace, research reveals that introverts excel in leadership roles. Introverts are skilled listeners and receptive to suggestions from proactive team members, making them effective leaders.

Introversion Versus Shyness

Introversion is often misunderstood, with many associating it with shyness and social reservation. Introversion and shyness are distinct concepts. While shyness is an emotion characterized by discomfort and anxiety in social situations, introversion is a personality type focused on a preference for solitude and smaller social groups. Introverts choose solitude for energizing purposes, not driven by negative reactions to larger gatherings.

Types of Introverts

Introversion is not a one-size-fits-all personality stamp; rather, it falls on a scale with variations. Research by psychologist Jonathan Cheek identifies four shades of introversion: social, thinking, anxious, and restrained. Social introversion involves a preference for small groups or solitude without social anxiety. Thinking introversion relates to introspection and imaginative creativity. Anxious introversion may lead to seeking solitude due to social anxiety. Restrained introversion involves a reserved and thoughtful approach, thinking before acting. Many individuals display a mix of these introverted types.

Understanding introversion goes beyond stereotypes, recognizing the diversity and strengths inherent in this personality type. Embracing introversion empowers individuals to navigate professional and personal spheres authentically.

Note: Toward the end of the book is a chapter *"Exploring the Spectrum: Introversion and Extraversion in Psychology and Beyond"* that elaborately explores the foundational roles of introversion and extraversion in shaping human personality, tracing their origins from Carl Jung's theory to their application in the MBTI and enrichment by Indian philosophical perspectives, providing a comprehensive overview of their impact on psychology and culture.

Famous Personalities Who Were Introverts

Introverts have long been overlooked in various domains, from entrepreneurship to politics. However, a closer look reveals that introverted personalities bring unique strengths and perspectives to the table, leading to significant successes in their respective fields.

Entrepreneurs:

Among the ranks of successful entrepreneurs, introverts have made their mark through their quiet determination and strategic thinking. Take, for instance, Amancio Ortega, the visionary behind Zara and other global fashion brands. Despite his reserved nature, Ortega's focus on simplicity and attention to detail has propelled him to the top of the fashion industry. In India, introverted entrepreneurs like Dhirubhai Ambani, the founder of Reliance Industries, and Narayana Murthy, the co-founder of Infosys, have also left an indelible mark on their respective industries. Despite their introverted tendencies, Ambani and Murthy demonstrated exceptional leadership skills and a knack for spotting opportunities, laying the foundations for their companies' phenomenal success.

Media and Entertainment Personalities:

A.R. Rahman, the renowned music composer, embarked on his musical journey at a tender age. His ground-breaking contributions to film music propelled him to fame, revolutionizing the Indian film industry with his innovative compositions. Despite achieving immense success and garnering widespread acclaim, Rahman is characterized by his introverted nature and humble demeanor. Similarly, Oprah Winfrey, a US media proprietor and talk show host has shattered expectations with her multifaceted media empire. Behind-the-scenes, Winfrey cherishes her privacy and moments of introspection, undoubtedly contributing to her unparalleled success in the entertainment industry.

Politicians:

In the domain of politics, introverts have demonstrated that quiet leadership can be just as effective as charismatic rhetoric. Former US President Barack Obama, known for his thoughtful and introspective approach to governance, exemplifies how introverts can make a profound impact on the world stage. Lal Bahadur Shastri, who served as Prime Minister of India, was known for his simplicity and humility. He was a man of few words but had a strong resolve and led by example. Mariano Rajoy, the former Prime Minister of Spain, navigated the complexities of politics with his reserved demeanor and prudent decision-making. Despite the pressures of public office, Rajoy remained true to his introverted nature, earning respect for his steadfast leadership.

Activists:

In the arena of activism, introverts have played pivotal roles in driving social change and advancing causes close to their hearts. Mahatma Gandhi, revered as the father of the Indian independence movement, embodied introverted principles of quiet strength and nonviolent resistance, inspiring millions to join his struggle for freedom. Likewise, Rosa Parks, often described as introverted and reserved, sparked a revolution with her simple act of defiance on a Montgomery bus. Despite facing immense pressure, Parks remained steadfast in her convictions, challenging systemic injustice, and paving the way for future generations.

Scientists:

In the realm of science, introverts have made ground-breaking discoveries through their deep contemplation and focus. Albert Einstein, renowned for his theory of relativity, epitomized the introverted scientist, finding solace in solitude and harnessing his inner thoughts to unlock the mysteries of the universe. Dr. A. P. J. Abdul Kalam, often referred to as the "Missile Man of India," was a renowned aerospace scientist who played a pivotal role in India's missile development programs. He was known for his humility, simplicity, and introspective personality. He preferred to focus on his work rather than seek the limelight, embodying the qualities of an introverted leader in the field of science and technology.

Introverted Sports Celebrities:

Even in the high-octane world of sports, introverts have thrived with their quiet determination and focused mindset. Rahul Dravid, the legendary Indian cricketer, honed his skills through relentless practice and introspection, proving that success on the field requires more than flashy moves. Michael Jordan, widely regarded as the greatest basketball player of all time, exemplified introverted qualities such as meticulous preparation and a relentless work ethic. Despite his fame, Jordan maintained a focused and disciplined approach to his craft, demonstrating that introverts can excel in even the most competitive arenas.

Introverted Writers:

In the world of literature, introverted writers like J.K. Rowling have captured the imaginations of millions with their introspective storytelling and nuanced characters. Rowling's journey from quiet introspection to global fame serves as a testament to the power of introversion in creative expression.

In conclusion, introverts have proven time and again that success knows no bounds when one embraces their true self. Whether in entrepreneurship, politics, activism, science, sports, or literature, introverted individuals have left an indelible mark on the world, reminding us that quiet strength and introspection can be powerful catalysts for change. As we celebrate their achievements, let us also recognize the value of introversion in a world that often prizes extroversion above all else.

Unveiling the Strengths of Introverts

Upon closer examination, it becomes evident that introverts possess a wealth of valuable qualities that contribute to their success in various aspects of life. Let's delve deeper into these strengths and explore how introverts can leverage them to excel in their lives.

Embracing Your Introversion

Contrary to popular belief, being an introvert is not a weakness; it is a superpower. Introverts possess a unique set of characteristics that set them apart, including exceptional listening skills, deep empathy, and the ability to think critically and reflect deeply. By embracing these qualities, introverts can tap into the power of introversion and make significant contributions in their workplace and beyond.

- **Exceptional Listening Skills:** Introverts excel in the art of active listening, paying close attention to what others say and processing information thoughtfully. This allows them to understand complex issues and perspectives more deeply, fostering better communication and collaboration in the workplace.

- **Deep Empathy:** Introverts often possess a heightened sense of empathy, allowing them to connect with others on a deeper level and understand their emotions and experiences. This empathetic nature enables introverts to build strong relationships and foster a supportive and inclusive work environment.

- **Critical Thinking and Reflection:** Introverts are natural deep thinkers who enjoy spending time in introspection and reflection. This introspective nature allows them to analyze situations thoroughly, identify underlying patterns and trends, and develop innovative solutions to complex problems.

Deep Focus and Creativity

One of the hallmarks of introverts is their ability to thrive in environments that allow for deep focus and uninterrupted work. Unlike their extroverted counterparts, who draw energy from social interactions, introverts find inspiration and creativity in solitude. By creating a workspace that fosters concentration and minimizing distractions, introverts can tap into their innate ability to think deeply and produce high-quality work.

- **Extended Focus:** Introverts have the remarkable ability to maintain focus for extended periods, allowing them to delve deeply into tasks and projects without getting distracted. This extended focus enables them to achieve high levels of productivity and produce work of exceptional quality.
- **Creativity in Solitude:** Introverts often find that their best ideas and creative insights emerge when they are alone with their thoughts. Solitude provides introverts with the mental space and freedom to explore new ideas, experiment with different approaches, and unleash their creative potential.
- **Thorough Exploration:** Introverts approach tasks and projects with meticulous attention to detail, thoroughly exploring every aspect and considering all possible angles. This thorough exploration ensures that they have a comprehensive understanding of the subject matter and can make well-informed decisions.

Effective Communication

Introverts are known for their excellent listening skills and thoughtful responses. In the workplace, introverts can leverage these strengths to become effective communicators. By actively listening to their colleagues and clients, introverts can gain a better understanding of their needs and provide thoughtful solutions. Additionally, introverts can communicate their ideas in a clear and concise manner, ensuring their message is heard and understood by others.

- **Active Listening:** Introverts excel in the art of active listening, focusing intently on what others say and processing information thoughtfully before responding. This active listening allows them to understand the needs, concerns, and perspectives of their colleagues and clients more deeply, fostering better communication and collaboration.

- **Thoughtful Communication:** Introverts take the time to carefully consider their words before speaking, ensuring that they communicate their ideas in a clear, concise, and impactful manner. This thoughtful communication style enables introverts to articulate their thoughts and opinions effectively, making them valuable contributors to team discussions and decision-making processes.

- **Clear and Concise Expression:** Introverts have a knack for distilling complex ideas and concepts into simple, easy-to-understand language. This clear and concise expression ensures that their message is communicated effectively and resonates with their audience, whether it's a colleague, client, or stakeholder.

Building Meaningful Connections

While introverts may prefer smaller social circles, they excel at building deep and meaningful connections with others. In the workplace, introverts can leverage their natural ability to connect with colleagues on a deeper level, fostering trust and collaboration. By seeking out one-on-one interactions and engaging in meaningful conversations, introverts can build strong professional relationships that enhance their success at work.

- **Quality over Quantity:** Introverts prioritize quality over quantity when it comes to relationships, investing time and energy in forming deep, personal connections with their colleagues. This focus on quality relationships fosters trust, loyalty, and mutual respect, creating a supportive and collaborative work environment.
- **Deep Understanding:** Introverts have a natural curiosity and desire to understand others on a deeper level, which allows them to build strong and meaningful connections. By asking thoughtful questions, actively listening, and empathizing with their colleagues, introverts can develop a deep understanding of their needs, motivations, and aspirations.
- **Building Trust:** Introverts are known for their integrity, honesty, and reliability, qualities that are essential for building trust in relationships. By consistently demonstrating their trustworthiness through their words and actions, introverts can earn the respect and admiration of their colleagues, paving the way for meaningful and lasting connections.

Self-Care and Recharging

Introverts are more sensitive to external stimuli and require time alone to recharge their energy. Recognizing the importance of self-care and setting boundaries is crucial for introverts to maintain their well-being and performance in the workplace. By incorporating regular breaks, quiet time, and activities that align with their interests, introverts can ensure they are operating at their best.

- **Importance of Self-Care:** Introverts recognize the importance of self-care and prioritize activities that promote their physical, mental, and emotional well-being. Whether it's taking a walk-in nature, practicing mindfulness meditation, or indulging in a favorite hobby, introverts understand the importance of carving out time for self-care amidst their busy schedules.

- **Setting Boundaries:** Introverts are mindful of their energy levels and know when to set boundaries to protect their time and resources. Whether it's saying no to additional commitments, delegating tasks to others, or scheduling regular breaks throughout the day, introverts understand the importance of preserving their energy and avoiding burnout.

- **Recharging in Solitude:** Introverts recharge their energy by spending time alone in solitude, away from the hustle and bustle of the outside world. Whether it's reading a book, listening to music, or simply enjoying peaceful reflection, introverts find solace and rejuvenation in moments of solitude.

Distinct Skills Setting Introverts Apart

In addition to these overarching strengths, introverts possess a set of distinct skills that set them apart from their extroverted counterparts. Let's delve into four of these unique qualities:

- **Gifted in Specific Fields:** Statistics reveal that a significant percentage of gifted individuals are introverts, excelling in specific domains such as music, art, or mathematics. This affinity for certain fields highlights the depth of talent introverts bring to areas where focused expertise is crucial.

- **Integrity and Moral Compass:** Introverts often exhibit a strong sense of integrity and an unwavering moral compass. Less swayed by external influences, they rely on their inner values, promoting ethical decision-making and establishing themselves as trustworthy individuals.

- **Critical Thinking with Thicker Gray Matter:** Studies suggest that introverts' brains exhibit thicker gray matter, contributing to enhanced critical thinking and rational thought. This cognitive advantage enables introverts to analyze situations thoroughly, make well-informed decisions, and navigate complex challenges with clarity.

- **Less Distraction:** The ability to maintain concentration is a notable strength of introverts, allowing them to deeply immerse in tasks and projects without distraction. This sustained attention results in high productivity and exceptional quality work.

In conclusion, introverts possess a myriad of strengths and skills that make them invaluable contributors in any setting. By recognizing and embracing these qualities, introverts can unlock their full potential and make meaningful contributions to their workplaces, communities, and beyond. It's time to celebrate the unique strengths of introverts and create environments that allow them to thrive.

Perceived Weaknesses of Introverts

Introverts bring valuable strengths to the workplace, but they also contend with certain perceived weaknesses that can impact their professional journey. Understanding and addressing these challenges is crucial for both introverts and their colleagues to foster a supportive and inclusive work environment. Let's delve deeper into five common perceived weaknesses of introverts:

The Desire for External Validation

Introverts may have a tendency to prioritize the approval of others over their own personal goals and priorities. This desire for external validation can sometimes lead introverts to compromise their own values or neglect their individual aspirations in favor of seeking acceptance from others. While seeking approval from colleagues or supervisors can be motivating, introverts must be mindful not to rely too heavily on external validation and instead focus on their intrinsic worth and personal growth.

Heightened Sensitivity

Introverts often possess a heightened sensitivity, which can manifest in various ways in the workplace. While sensitivity enables introverts to empathize with others and perceive nuances in their environment, it can also make them more susceptible to criticism and feedback. Introverts may take feedback personally or dwell on negative comments, potentially hindering their ability to learn and grow from constructive criticism. By embracing their sensitivity as a strength rather than a weakness, introverts can cultivate resilience and develop strategies for processing feedback in a constructive manner.

Anxiety in Certain Situations

Introverts may experience anxiety in certain social or high-pressure situations, such as networking events, presentations, or performance reviews. The prospect of interacting with unfamiliar colleagues or speaking in front of a large audience can trigger feelings of discomfort or apprehension for introverts, leading to heightened anxiety levels. This anxiety may manifest in physical symptoms such as sweating, trembling, or rapid heartbeat, further exacerbating the introvert's discomfort. To navigate this challenge, introverts can develop coping mechanisms and relaxation techniques to manage their anxiety effectively.

Struggle with Interruptions

Introverts are often easily distracted by external stimuli, which can pose challenges in environments with constant interruptions or noise. Open office layouts, frequent meetings, or noisy work environments may disrupt an introvert's concentration and impede their ability to focus on tasks or projects. This struggle with interruptions can hinder the introvert's productivity and lead to feelings of frustration or overwhelm. Introverts may benefit from creating a quiet and distraction-free workspace, establishing clear boundaries around their time and availability, and advocating for their need for focused concentration.

Quietness or Unassertiveness

Introverts may adopt a quieter demeanor in meetings or group settings, which can sometimes lead to their contributions being overlooked or overshadowed by more vocal colleagues. In discussions or brainstorming sessions, introverts may hesitate to speak up or assert themselves, preferring to listen and reflect on their thoughts before sharing them with others. This quietness or unassertiveness can sometimes be misinterpreted as disinterest or lack of confidence, leading to the introvert's ideas or perspectives being undervalued or dismissed. To address this challenge, introverts can practice assertiveness techniques, such as speaking up with confidence and clarity and advocating for their ideas and opinions in a respectful and assertive manner. Additionally, creating a culture of inclusivity and respect where all voices are valued and encouraged can empower introverts to express themselves authentically and make meaningful contributions to team discussions and decision-making processes.

In conclusion, while introverts may face certain perceived weaknesses in the workplace, they also possess a unique set of strengths and qualities that make them valuable contributors to any team. By acknowledging and addressing these challenges, introverts and their colleagues can create a supportive and inclusive work environment where everyone can thrive and contribute to the organization's success.

 **Chapter highlights:**

- Introversion is not a one-size-fits-all personality stamp. It's a complex trait with variations, encompassing different behaviors, preferences, and strengths. It goes beyond stereotypes, acknowledging the diversity within the introverted spectrum.

- Through the examples, you saw how introverted individuals have achieved remarkable success in various fields. Qualities such as introspection, determination, and focus, which are inherent in introversion, can be powerful assets in driving innovation, leadership, and social change.

- Embrace the unique qualities of introversion, such as exceptional listening skills, deep empathy, and critical thinking abilities, as valuable assets that contribute to success in various aspects of life. By embracing these strengths, introverts can excel in their personal and professional lives and celebrate introversion as a valuable asset.

- Introverts face challenges such as a desire for external validation, heightened sensitivity, anxiety in certain situations, struggle with interruptions, and quietness or unassertiveness. Recognizing and addressing these challenges is essential for introverts and their colleagues to foster a supportive work environment.

Chapter 3

The Challenges of Being an Introvert in the Workplace

Navigating the intricacies of the modern workplace can pose significant challenges for introverted individuals. In this chapter, we delve into the common hurdles faced by introverts as they navigate professional environments. Despite possessing a unique set of strengths and qualities that can enrich team dynamics and foster innovation, introverts often find themselves grappling with obstacles that hinder their progress and impede their ability to thrive. By shedding light on these challenges and their potential negative impacts on introverted employees, we aim to empower individuals to overcome barriers and leverage their inherent strengths to excel in their respective roles.

Common Challenges Faced by Introverts in the Workplace

Introverts possess a unique set of strengths and qualities that can greatly contribute to a productive and successful workplace. However, they often face various challenges that can hinder their progress and ability to thrive in a work environment. Understanding these challenges is crucial for introvert employees to overcome them and excel in their respective roles.

Networking and Socializing Drains Energy

Introverts often find the process of networking and socializing in professional settings to be physically and mentally draining, unlike their extroverted counterparts. This is attributed to their intrinsic need for solitude and limited social stimulation. Engaging in the expected social interactions, such as attending networking events or participating in team building activities, can be energy-consuming for introverts. Implications:

- **Energy Drain:** Social interactions may exhaust introverts, impacting their overall energy levels.
- **Hindered Engagement:** The need for solitude may hinder their ability to fully engage in social gatherings, potentially affecting relationship building.
- **Challenges in Expression:** Expressing themselves confidently during meetings or presentations becomes challenging as introverts tend to focus internally on their thoughts rather than outwardly on the on-going conversation.

Increased Risk of Feeling Overwhelmed

Introverts possess a heightened sensitivity to external stimuli, including noise and chaotic environments. This sensitivity makes them more susceptible to feeling overwhelmed in situations with high levels of stimulation, such as busy offices or crowded events. The overwhelming nature of these environments can lead to increased anxiety and stress for introverts. Implications:

- **Stress and Anxiety:** Overwhelming situations can contribute to heightened stress and anxiety levels among introverts.
- **Impact on Coping Mechanisms:** The difficulty in coping with various situations may affect their overall well-being and ability to perform optimally in challenging environments.

The Tendency Toward Overthinking and Ruminating

Introverts, known for their reflective and deep-thinking nature, may exhibit a tendency toward overthinking and ruminating. When faced with challenges or decisions, introverts may get stuck on one train of thought, leading to negative thinking patterns. This propensity for deep contemplation can contribute to increased stress and anxiety levels. Implications:

- **Negative Thought Patterns:** Overthinking can lead to negative thought patterns, potentially impacting mental health.
- **Increased Stress:** The constant analysis of situations may contribute to heightened stress and anxiety levels.
- **Overthinking:** Overthinking can hinder swift decision-making, posing challenges in time-sensitive scenarios.

Struggle with Assertiveness and Standing Up for Oneself

Introverts often lean toward a more passive communication style, making it challenging for them to express themselves confidently or assertively. This passivity may hinder their ability to stand up for their beliefs when faced with opposition or challenges. Additionally, introverts may experience hesitation and discomfort when required to speak up spontaneously. Implications:

- **Difficulty in Expression:** Struggling with assertiveness can limit their ability to express ideas and opinions confidently.
- **Challenges in Opposition:** Facing opposition may be more challenging for introverts who may be hesitant to confront or disagree with others.
- **Discomfort in Spontaneity:** Introverts may feel uncomfortable when put on the spot, affecting their ability to respond spontaneously.

Difficulty in Verbal Communication and Decision-Making

Introverts may encounter difficulties in verbal communication, especially in situations that demand quick responses. Their tendency to take more time to process thoughts can impact their ability to express themselves verbally on the spot. This challenge extends to decision-making, where introverts may require additional time for thorough analysis. Implications:

- **Communication Hurdles:** Verbal communication challenges can lead to difficulty expressing thoughts and ideas in real time.

- **Impact on Meetings and Interviews:** Meetings, interviews, and casual conversations may be affected, as introverts may take more time to articulate their responses.

- **Challenges in Decision-Making:** Decision-making under time constraints can be challenging, affecting their responsiveness in fast-paced scenarios.

Struggle with Self-Promotion:

Introverts often struggle with self-promotion and advocating for themselves in the workplace. They may find it challenging to showcase their achievements and skills, which can hinder their career progression. Implications:

- **Missed Opportunities:** Without effective self-promotion, introverts may miss out on recognition for their contributions and opportunities for career advancement.

- **Underestimation of Skills:** Colleagues and supervisors may underestimate introverts' abilities and potential due to their reluctance to self-promote, leading to missed opportunities for challenging assignments or promotions.

- **Lack of Visibility:** Introverts' aversion to self-promotion may result in their work going unnoticed or undervalued, leading to limited visibility within the organization.
- **Stagnation in Career Growth:** The inability to effectively promote themselves may result in introverts becoming stuck in their current roles or experiencing slower career progression compared to their more vocal counterparts.
- **Difficulty in Expanding Professional Relationships:** Networking is essential for career development, but introverts may struggle to promote themselves and build professional relationships, limiting their access to opportunities and support networks.
- **Impact on Personal Brand:** Without effective self-promotion, introverts may struggle to develop a strong personal brand and differentiate themselves in a competitive job market.

To address these challenges, introverts should focus on highlighting their strengths and accomplishments through written communication or seeking support from mentors or advocates who can help promote their work. Developing a personal brand and leveraging their unique qualities can also help introverts stand out in an extroverted-dominated workplace.

By understanding and addressing these common challenges, introverted employees can unlock their full potential and excel in the workplace. Embracing their introverted nature, advocating for their needs, and leveraging their unique strengths will enable introverts to accelerate their success and contribute to a more balanced and inclusive work environment. This book provides further insights and practical strategies for introverts to thrive in their professional lives.

An Introvert's Silent Battle

In the heart of a bustling corporate office towered by glass and steel, Naina sat secluded in her cubicle, surrounded by piles of reports and spreadsheets. Her analytical skills were unmatched, her insights profound, yet in the cacophony of the corporate world, her voice, soft and hesitant, often went unheard.

The company, JYC, thrived on assertiveness and visibility. Here, ideas were less about substance and more about the showmanship with which they were presented. In this world, Vishal, Naina's extroverted counterpart, was king. His presentations were less about the numbers and more about the performance, a fact that didn't go unnoticed but was nonetheless celebrated.

One day, a high-profile project was announced, one that Naina had silently longed to work on. She knew her capabilities were perfect for the task. Yet, when the team was assembled, her name was conspicuously absent. Instead, Vishal was at the helm, his team composed of similarly extroverted personalities, their laughter and loud discussions often permeating the quiet of Naina's corner.

Feeling overlooked, Naina mustered the courage to speak to her supervisor, Pankaj, a man whose career was built on bold decisions and even bolder declarations.

"Pankaj," Naina began, her voice barely above a whisper, "I noticed the new project team was announced. I believe I have the right skills and could contribute significantly."

Pankaj, peering over his glasses, replied, "Naina, your work is indeed excellent. However, these roles require leadership and visibility. You do excellent work, but you're... how do I put this... a bit too quiet. We need someone who can be the face of the project, who can push forward in meetings and presentations."

Disheartened, Naina nodded, her fears confirmed. Her introversion, it seemed, was a barrier too high to climb in the eyes of her supervisors. She returned to her desk, the sounds of her colleagues' successes echoing around her, a stark reminder of what she perceived as her own invisibility.

Weeks turned into months, and Naina watched as promotions and opportunities passed her by, always to those more vocal, more visible. Her contributions, though significant, remained in the background, and her name was seldom mentioned in the corridors of recognition. It wasn't just the projects or the promotions; it was the daily meetings where her ideas, softly spoken, were steamrolled by louder voices, only to be repeated by someone else and met with applause.

The annual review sealed her silent fears. "Needs to be more visible and assertive," read the feedback, a refrain as familiar as it was frustrating. The consequences of her reserved nature were laid bare: limited promotion opportunities missed assignments, and a salary that barely budged, a stark contrast to her more extroverted peers.

In the solitude of her cubicle, Naina couldn't help but wonder about the countless others like her, whose talents simmered in silence, overshadowed by the dazzle of extroversion. The corporate landscape, with its unspoken biases, seemed an arena ill-fitted for the introspective, the contemplative, the quietly brilliant.

As the office lights dimmed, Naina remained, her thoughts lost in the reports in front of her, a silent testament to the quiet battles fought and often lost within the gleaming facades of corporate giants.

Negative impacts that Introverts may experience in their career

Introverts often face unique challenges in the workplace due to their reserved nature. If they are unwilling to adapt to certain extroverted behavioral tactics, they may encounter several repercussions. Here are some of the negative impacts introverts may experience in the workplace:

- **Limited Promotion Opportunities:** Introverts may miss out on promotions because of their reluctance to self-promote. They may not actively seek leadership roles, resulting in their talents going unrecognized by management.

- **Reduced Salary Increases:** Introverts may receive smaller salary increases compared to extroverts who are more assertive in negotiating for higher compensation. Their low visibility may lead to their contributions being undervalued during salary review processes.

- **Missed Good Assignments:** Due to their quiet demeanor, introverts may not be considered for high-profile projects. They may not actively seek opportunities to showcase their skills, leading to their talents being overlooked by managers and colleagues.

- **Lack of Recognition:** Introverts may not receive the recognition they deserve for their hard work and achievements. Their contributions may be overshadowed by more outgoing colleagues who are adept at self-promotion.

- **Limited Network:** Introverts may struggle to build strong professional networks due to discomfort with socializing. This may result in missed career opportunities and mentorship.

- **Stagnation in Career Growth:** Reluctance to step outside their comfort zones may lead to stagnation in career growth. Introverts may be hesitant to seek out opportunities for advancement, limiting their upward mobility.

- **Difficulty in Leadership Roles:** Introverts may be overlooked for leadership positions due to stereotypes about extroverted qualities. Despite possessing valuable leadership qualities, introverts may struggle to assert themselves in a workplace culture that values extroversion.

- **Negative Performance Evaluations:** Introverts perceived as lacking in extroverted behaviors may receive negative performance evaluations. This can damage their self-esteem and hinder professional development.

Overall, introverts may face significant challenges in the workplace due to their introverted nature. It's important for organizations to recognize and value the unique contributions of introverted employees and create inclusive work environments that support their professional growth and development. While introverts should remain true to themselves, adapting to certain behaviors can benefit their careers. Finding a balance between authenticity and adaptability is essential for introverts to thrive in diverse work environments. By leveraging their unique strengths and embracing opportunities for growth, introverts can overcome workplace challenges and achieve success.

 **Chapter highlights:**

- Introverts face several challenges in the workplace, including networking exhaustion, heightened sensitivity leading to feeling overwhelmed, a tendency toward overthinking and passivity, difficulty in verbal communication and self-promotion, and struggles with assertiveness. Recognizing and addressing these challenges is essential for introverts to thrive in their professional roles.

- Introverts may encounter various negative impacts in their career, including limited promotion opportunities, reduced salary increases, missed assignments, lack of recognition, networking difficulties, career stagnation, leadership barriers, and negative performance evaluations. These challenges stem from their reserved nature and reluctance to engage in extroverted behaviors, which may hinder their professional growth and development.

Step Out of Your Comfort Zone

Introverts face unique challenges that can impact their success. While introverts should remain true to themselves, adapting to certain behaviors can benefit their careers. Finding a balance between authenticity and adaptability is essential for introverts to thrive in diverse work environments. By leveraging their unique strengths and embracing opportunities for growth, introverts can overcome workplace challenges and achieve success.

The seven steps identified here serve as your guide on this journey, empowering you to emerge victorious in the professional realm while staying true to your introverted nature. One of the common themes across the seven action steps for introverts to navigate their journey toward success is to recognize and leverage their Introvert's strengths. From embracing their introversion to building confidence, effective communication, networking, teamwork, leadership, and sustaining long-term success, each step offers valuable strategies for introverts to thrive in their professional lives.

The seven steps are:

- Step 1: Leveraging Introvert Strengths
- Step 2: Building Confidence
- Step 3: Effective Communication
- Step 4: Networking and Relationship Building
- Step 5: Teamwork and Collaboration
- Step 6: Strategies for Introvert Leadership
- Step 7: Sustaining Long-Term Success as an Introver

Step 1: Leveraging Introvert Strengths

"Diving into the depths of my abilities, I unearth the treasures that set me apart, ready to shine in the spotlight."

In step 1 of your journey, we delve into the core strengths inherent to introverted individuals, unlocking the potential that lies within your unique disposition. Through honing active listening and observational skills, you harness the power of perception, delving beyond surface interactions to grasp the subtleties of human communication. Your analytical prowess and adept problem-solving abilities serve as pillars of strength, enabling you to navigate complex challenges with finesse and precision. Moreover, your innate creativity and capacity for innovation fuel transformative ideas, reshaping paradigms and fostering progress. Embracing self-reflective practices, you cultivate a deeper understanding of yourself, paving the way for personal growth and professional fulfillment. Together, these strengths form the bedrock upon which you can build a path to success, harnessing your inherent capabilities to thrive in any endeavor you pursue.

A quiet, serene lake reflecting the sky, symbolizing introspection, and deep-thinking qualities of introverts, portraying their inner world as a source of strength.

Why Should You Leverage Your Strengths?

As an introvert you possess inherent strengths such as exceptional listening skills, critical thinking abilities, creativity, and innovation. By leveraging these skills and employing specific strategies, introverts can accelerate their success in the workplace. Embracing their introverted nature and capitalizing on their unique abilities will not only benefit their careers but also contribute to the overall success of their organizations.

Active Listening and Observational Skills

One of the most powerful tools in an introvert's arsenal is active listening. In a world of noise and distractions, the ability to truly listen is a rare and valuable skill. But have you ever stopped to consider just how impactful this skill can be? Active listening goes beyond just hearing words; it's about understanding the emotions, intentions, and underlying messages behind them. For introverts, mastering this art can forge stronger connections with colleagues, build trust, and unveil invaluable insights crucial for professional growth.

Observational skills are another inherent strength of introverts. Naturally inclined to observe and analyze their surroundings, introverts excel at picking up on subtle cues and details others might overlook. It's like having a superpower, isn't it? By honing these observational skills, introverts become indispensable in the workplace, identifying patterns, anticipating problems, and offering unique perspectives that lead to innovative solutions. Their attention to detail showcases dedication and reliability, earning the trust and respect of peers and superiors alike.

It's crucial for introverts to recognize and embrace these unique strengths. By actively listening and sharpening observational skills, they can navigate the workplace with confidence and achieve remarkable success. Remember, introversion isn't a weakness—it's a powerful asset waiting to be unleashed. So, fellow introverts, it's time to tap into that inner strength and soar to new heights in the workplace.

Analytical Thinking and Problem-Solving Abilities

Amidst the rapid pace and fierce competitive work environment, possessing strong analytical thinking and problem-solving abilities has become an essential skill set for all employees. For introverts, who often thrive in quiet and reflective environments, developing these skills can be particularly advantageous in accelerating their success at the workplace.

Analytical thinking is like unraveling a complex puzzle, isn't it? It's about processing information, spotting patterns, and weaving logical connections to craft well-informed decisions. And who better than introverts to excel in this arena? With their penchant for deep contemplation and meticulous attention to detail, introverts naturally gravitate toward analytical thinking. They have this knack for dissecting intricate problems, breaking them down into bite-sized pieces, and examining each fragment with thoughtful precision. It's like watching a master craftsman at work, methodically chiseling away until the perfect solution emerges.

Now, problem-solving. That's where introverts truly shine. They're like detectives, meticulously combing through every clue, exploring every angle until they unearth the hidden truth. Their preference for solitude and introspection gives them this unique ability to dive deep into the heart of an issue, uncovering insights and perspectives that others might miss. It's almost like they have this secret key to unlock the door to innovative solutions.

Even introverts need a little boost sometimes. Creating a quiet, focused work environment can do wonders for their cognitive prowess. Minimizing distractions and finding that perfect spot to think can really help introverts concentrate and process information more effectively. And let's not forget about journaling or meditation—those practices can really amp up their introspective game, sharpening their analytical skills to a razor's edge.

Now, collaboration might not be an introvert's first instinct, but it's like mixing different colors on a palette to create a masterpiece. By actively participating in group discussions and sharing their unique perspectives, introverts can infuse their analytical thinking into a collective brainstorming process. It's about finding that delicate balance between solitude and collaboration. By embracing both sides of the coin, introverts can contribute their creative ideas to team projects while still honoring their need for reflection. After all, innovation is a dance between the individual and the collective, and introverts bring their own unique rhythm to the table.

Creativity and Innovation

The ability to foster creativity and innovation is indeed essential for success, isn't it? While extroverted traits such as confidence and assertiveness are often associated with these qualities, introverts possess unique strengths that can accelerate their success.

Understanding the Introvert Advantage: Introverts possess a deep sense of introspection and an ability to think deeply, allowing them to generate unique and profound insights. By embracing their preference for solitude and quiet reflection, introverts can harness their creativity in ways that extroverts may struggle with.

Creating an Optimal Environment: Introverts thrive in calm and quiet environments, away from distractions. Understanding this, introverted employees can create conducive workspaces that promote focus and concentration. By minimizing interruptions and creating structured routines, introverts can cultivate an environment that nurtures their creativity and allows them to generate innovative ideas.

Harnessing the Power of Introverted Thinking: Introverts often excel at deep analysis and reflection, which are crucial components of the creative process. By embracing their natural inclination toward introspection, introvert employees can engage in activities like journaling, brainstorming, and mind mapping to stimulate their creativity.

Embracing Failure and Iteration: Creativity and innovation often involve taking risks and embracing failure as a learning opportunity. Introverts may be more cautious by nature, but this chapter will encourage them to step out of their comfort zones and embrace the iterative process of creativity. By reframing failure as a stepping stone to success and adopting a growth mindset, introverts can overcome their fear of failure and unlock their full creative potential.

Creativity and innovation are truly the lifeblood of any successful organization. And here's the thing—these qualities aren't exclusive to extroverts. Introvert employees bring their own set of unique strengths to the table. By tapping into and harnessing these introverted traits, they have the power to drive innovation and make significant contributions to their teams and organizations.

Self-Reflective Practices

The Power of Introspection

Self-reflective practices play a pivotal role in the journey of an introvert. These practices enable individuals to understand their strengths, preferences, and areas for growth, paving the way for a more authentic and fulfilling life.

Journaling

Keeping a journal allows introverts to capture their thoughts, feelings, and reflections. Journaling provides a private space for introspection, helping introverts gain clarity on their values and aspirations.

Mindfulness and Meditation

Practicing mindfulness and meditation allows introverts to cultivate a heightened awareness of the present moment. These techniques aid in managing stress, enhancing self-awareness, and fostering a sense of inner peace.

Personality Assessments

Engaging in personality assessments, such as the Myers-Briggs Type Indicator (MBTI) or the Big Five Personality Traits, provides introverts with valuable insights into their preferences and tendencies. Understanding one's personality type can be a powerful tool for self-discovery.

Navigating the Journey of Self-Discovery

Embracing Individuality

Self-discovery involves embracing one's individuality, including the introverted traits that contribute to a unique blend of strengths. Introverts should celebrate their unique qualities rather than viewing them as impediments.

Setting Authentic Goals

Understanding personal strengths and preferences empowers introverts to set goals aligned with their authentic selves. This process ensures that aspirations are not driven by external expectations but rooted in genuine desires.

Building Resilience

Self-reflective practices contribute to building resilience. Introverts, armed with a deep understanding of themselves, can navigate challenges with grace, drawing strength from their internal reservoir of insights and self-awareness.

Embracing introversion is a transformative journey that involves recognizing the beauty of one's unique traits and engaging in self-reflective practices for personal growth. As introverts navigate this path of self-discovery, they contribute immeasurable value to various aspects of life, enriching the world with their creativity, empathy, and thoughtful contributions. The power of embracing introversion lies not just in understanding oneself but in leveraging these inherent qualities to create a meaningful and fulfilling life journey.

Quick exercise:

Take a moment to reflect on the strengths and unique abilities that you bring to the table. Write down the top five of them in the space provided below:

1.

2.

3.

4.

5.

Now, consider these strengths and capabilities and acknowledge the value you bring to your team, organization, and community. Recognize the significance of your contributions and the impact you make through your talents and skills.

Are you leveraging your Introvert Strengths?

Self-assessment

Take this self-assessment. Rate each of the statements on a scale of 1 to 5. Please choose the number that best represents your feelings, thoughts, and behaviors.

Less True 1   2   3   4   5 More True

S.No.	Statement	Your response
1	I actively listen to others, seeking to understand their perspectives before sharing my own.	
2	I often notice details and patterns that others overlook.	
3	I enjoy analyzing complex problems and finding innovative solutions.	
4	I prefer quiet and focused work environments.	
5	I am comfortable with solitude and introspection.	
6	I often reflect on my thoughts, feelings, and experiences.	
7	I believe failure is a valuable learning opportunity.	
8	I enjoy generating new ideas and thinking creatively.	
9	I am open to trying new approaches, even if they involve risk.	
10	I celebrate my unique qualities and appreciate the strengths of introversion.	

Scoring: Please add up all 'Your responses' and review your score in the Score Key.

Score Key

Score Interpretation: Here's what your score might indicate:

- Total Score 40-50: You are effectively leveraging your introvert strengths. Keep up the great work!
- Total Score 30-39: You are on the right track but may benefit from further developing some aspects of leveraging your introvert strengths.
- Total Score 20-29: There is room for improvement in leveraging your introvert strengths. Consider focusing on areas where you scored lower.
- Total Score 10-19: You may not be fully leveraging your introvert strengths. Identifying and embracing these strengths can enhance your success and satisfaction in the workplace.

Step 2: Building Confidence

"Each step forward is a declaration of my worth,
forging an unbreakable shield against doubt and uncertainty."

In step 2, embark on a transformative journey to fortify your confidence as an introvert, empowering yourself to thrive in any situation. By embracing self-awareness, you embark on a voyage of self-discovery, gaining insight into your strengths, weaknesses, and unique qualities. Through the cultivation of a growth mindset, you unlock the potential for continuous learning and development, reframing challenges as opportunities for growth. Confront impostor syndrome head-on, banishing self-doubt and embracing your worthiness and capabilities. Finally, nurture introvert confidence, harnessing the power of authenticity and self-assurance to navigate the complexities of the world with poise and resilience. As you embark on this empowering journey, you lay the foundation for personal and professional success, emboldened by the unwavering belief in your abilities as an introvert.

A sapling thriving in a unique environment symbolizing resilience and the growth of confidence in challenging situations.

Why Should You Build Confidence?

By overcoming the 'impostor syndrome' through self-acceptance, reframing thoughts, seeking support, adopting a growth mindset, and celebrating achievements, you as an introvert can accelerate your success and unleash your inner strength to excel in your careers. (Impostor syndrome is a psychological phenomenon in which individuals doubt their abilities, talents, or achievements.)

Embracing Self-Awareness

Introverts often find themselves struggling to navigate the workplace. However, introverts possess a unique set of strengths that can be harnessed to achieve remarkable success. To tap into this potential, it is crucial for introvert employees to embrace self-awareness – a skill that will empower them to excel in the workplace and accelerate their success.

Self-awareness is the foundation upon which introverts can build their professional journey. Understanding one's own temperament and preferences is like unlocking a hidden treasure trove. It allows introverts to identify their strengths and weaknesses, empowering them to leverage their natural inclinations to their advantage. This self-awareness not only leads to increased job satisfaction but also fosters a sense of fulfillment.

One key aspect of introverts' self-awareness is recognizing their need for solitude and introspection. Unlike extroverts who thrive in social interactions, introverts recharge and gain energy from quiet and solitary environments. It's like finding that perfect oasis amidst the hustle and bustle of the workplace. By acknowledging this fundamental aspect of their personality, introverted employees can proactively create a work environment that supports their needs. Whether it's carving out dedicated alone time or finding a quiet space to retreat when overwhelmed, these moments of solitude are like fuel for introverts, enhancing their productivity and preventing burnout.

Additionally, self-awareness allows introverts to understand how they communicate and collaborate with others. Introverts often excel in one-on-one interactions and are thoughtful listeners. It's like they have this innate ability to dive deep into conversations, doesn't it? By recognizing these strengths, introverted employees can leverage their ability to build deep connections and engage in meaningful conversations. When it comes to stepping out of their comfort zones, like presenting in front of larger groups, self-awareness helps introverts identify areas for growth and take proactive steps to develop those skills.

Furthermore, self-awareness empowers introverts to advocate for their own needs in the workplace. By understanding their limits and boundaries, introverts can effectively communicate their preferences to their colleagues and managers. It's about finding that balance between asserting oneself and respecting others. Whether it's asking for quieter workspaces or suggesting alternative approaches to team collaboration, introverts can create an environment that allows them to thrive and contribute their best work.

In conclusion, embracing self-awareness is a critical step for introverted employees seeking to excel in the workplace. It's like having a guiding compass. With self-awareness as their ally, introverts have the power to shape their work environment, communicate effectively, and leverage their unique abilities. And with each step forward, they're not just accelerating their success—they're paving the way for a fulfilling professional journey.

Developing a Growth Mindset

Introverts often face unique challenges that can hinder their success. However, with the right mindset and strategies, introverted employees have the power to not only excel but also accelerate their success.

A growth mindset is the belief that abilities and intelligence can be developed through dedication and hard work. This mindset embraces challenges, persists in the face of setbacks, and views failures as opportunities for growth. For introverted employees, cultivating a growth mindset can be a game-changer, helping them navigate the workplace with confidence and resilience.

One of the key aspects of developing a growth mindset is embracing challenges. Introverts may tend to avoid situations that push them out of their comfort zones. However, by reframing challenges as opportunities for growth, introverts can unlock their potential. A practical strategy to step out of your comfort zones is to set small, achievable goals or to seek support from mentors or colleagues.

Another crucial element is reframing failures. Introverts might be prone to dwelling on their mistakes or setbacks, which can hinder their progress. By adopting a growth mindset, introverts can view failures as valuable learning experiences and develop resilience. Ways to bounce back from failures include practicing self-compassion, seeking feedback, and focusing on growth rather than perfection.

We should not underestimate the power of effort and perseverance. Many introverts possess a strong work ethic and dedication to their tasks. By embracing a growth mindset, introverts can channel their determination and hard work into continuous improvement and professional development. To foster a strong work ethic, one can set clear goals, create a growth-oriented environment, and seek continuous learning opportunities.

Ultimately, developing a growth mindset empowers introverted employees to overcome obstacles and achieve their full potential. By embracing challenges, reframing failures, and persevering with effort, introverts can accelerate their success in the workplace.

Overcoming Impostor Syndrome

Impostor Syndrome, a phenomenon where individuals doubt their accomplishments and fear being exposed as a fraud, is a common struggle for many introverts in the workplace. It can hinder their progress, limit their potential, and prevent them from truly excelling in their careers. However, with the right strategies and mindset, introverts can overcome impostor syndrome and unleash their inner strengths to achieve remarkable success.

One of the first steps to overcoming impostor syndrome is to acknowledge and accept your achievements. As introverts, we tend to downplay our accomplishments and attribute them to luck or external factors. It is crucial to recognize that our skills, talents, and hard work have contributed to our success. Embrace your achievements and give yourself credit where it is due.

Another effective strategy is to reframe your thoughts. Instead of focusing on your perceived shortcomings or failures, shift your attention to your strengths and past accomplishments. Remind yourself of the times when you have excelled, overcome challenges, and received recognition for your work. This positive self-talk can help to build confidence and combat feelings of inadequacy.

Moreover, seeking support from trusted mentors and colleagues can be immensely helpful. Share your feelings of self-doubt and impostor syndrome with them. Not only will they provide reassurance and encouragement, but they can also offer valuable insights and perspectives. Remember, you are not alone in your struggles, and others have likely experienced similar feelings and insecurities.

Additionally, developing a growth mindset is crucial for overcoming impostor syndrome. Embrace challenges as opportunities for growth and learning rather than as threats to your competence. Understand that no one knows everything, and it is natural to make mistakes and learn from them. Cultivate a willingness to step out of your comfort zone, take on new responsibilities, and continuously improve your skills.

Finally, celebrate your achievements, no matter how small they may seem. Acknowledge the progress you have made, the skills you have developed, and the impact you have created. By recognizing and celebrating your wins, you reinforce your self-worth and build resilience against impostor syndrome.

Quick exercise:

Take a moment to celebrate your achievements by writing down five accomplishments that you are proud of. These accomplishments may include times when you excelled, overcame challenges, or received recognition for your work. Fill in the space provided below:

1.

2.

3.

4.

5.

Now, reflect on these accomplishments and engage in positive self-talk to build confidence whenever you need it. Acknowledge your successes and the resilience you've shown in reaching your goals.

Self-Talk Example:

Today, I'm taking a moment to acknowledge and celebrate my achievements. I've come so far and worked so hard to reach my goals. Let's look at the accomplishments I'm especially proud of:

- *Leading a Successful Project: I successfully led a project that not only met but exceeded our initial goals. This was a significant challenge, and I managed it with skill and dedication.*

- *Overcoming Public Speaking Anxiety: I overcame my fear of public speaking by presenting our quarterly results in front of the entire department. Each presentation feels a bit easier now, and I'm growing more confident in my abilities.*

- *Earning a Professional Certification: I studied diligently for several months and earned a certification that has added value to my skills and my resume. This achievement has opened new opportunities for my career growth.*

- *Receiving a Positive Performance Review: My hard work was recognized in my annual review, where I received high praise from my manager. This recognition is a testament to my commitment and effort.*

- *Volunteering for a Challenging Task: I volunteered to take on a new, challenging task at work that required learning new software. I mastered it quicker than expected, which significantly improved our team's efficiency.*

Reflecting on these accomplishments reminds me of my capability and adaptability. I am competent, I am resilient, and I am continually growing. These successes prove that I have what it takes to tackle new challenges and excel. I will keep pushing forward, using these achievements as a foundation for future successes. I am proud of what I've achieved, and I am excited about what I can accomplish next.

Building Your Confidence as an Introvert: Navigating the Journey to Assurance

As an introvert, you may find yourself grappling with the need to assert yourself confidently. The strategies below are tailored to enhance your self-confidence, providing practical tips to empower you to navigate professional and personal challenges with greater confidence. It's also crucial to understand, recognize, and appreciate traits commonly associated with introversion, which forms the foundation for building confidence tailored to your introverted strengths.

Strategies for Building Your Self-Confidence

- ✓ Positive Affirmations: Embrace positive affirmations tailored to your unique qualities. Affirmations focusing on strengths, such as deep thinking and empathetic listening, help build a positive self-image.
- ✓ Set Achievable Goals: Break down larger goals into smaller, achievable tasks. Celebrate small victories to contribute to a sense of accomplishment, reinforcing your self-assurance.
- ✓ Preparation and Planning: Thrive when well-prepared. Encourage meticulous preparation for tasks, whether it's a presentation or a professional challenge. Being thoroughly prepared mitigates anxiety and boosts your self-assurance.
- ✓ Focus on Your Individual Contributions: Highlight the value of your individual contributions. You often excel in thoughtful, well-considered contributions. Emphasizing the importance of your unique style reinforces your confidence in your abilities.
- ✓ Seek Feedback Strategically: Seek feedback selectively, focusing on constructive insights rather than seeking constant validation. Thoughtful feedback contributes to your growth and builds confidence over time.
- ✓ Visualization Techniques: Visualization can be a powerful tool for you. Visualize successful outcomes, whether it's acing a presentation or confidently navigating a social situation. This mental rehearsal enhances your confidence in real-life scenarios.

Actions for You to Take:

In these activities, you will engage with various aspects of positive psychology to enhance your self-confidence. Each action is designed to be practical and impactful, encouraging you to reflect on your strengths, set achievable goals, and develop a proactive mindset.

- Positive Affirmations: Create a list of affirmations highlighting your strengths and positive qualities. Write them on sticky notes and place them in visible locations around your workspace, such as your computer monitor or desk. Seeing these affirmations regularly serves as a constant reminder of your value and capabilities, boosting your confidence and self-image over time.

- Set Achievable Goals: Break down your larger goals into smaller, actionable steps. Create a visual representation of your goals using a planner, calendar, or goal-tracking app. Set aside dedicated time each day or week to work toward these smaller tasks, ticking them off as you accomplish them. Celebrate each milestone reached, no matter how small, to reinforce your sense of achievement and progress.

- Preparation and Planning: Allocate time in your schedule specifically for preparation and planning. Create a checklist or outline detailing the steps needed to prepare for upcoming tasks or challenges. Gather any necessary resources or materials well in advance. Set aside a quiet, uninterrupted space where you can focus solely on preparing for the task at hand. By thoroughly preparing and planning, you'll feel more confident and capable when it's time to tackle the challenge.

- Focus on Your Individual Contributions: Keep a journal or document where you record your individual contributions to projects or discussions. Take note of instances where your unique skills or strengths made a positive impact. Reflect on these contributions regularly to remind yourself of the value you bring to your team or organization. Sharing these successes with trusted colleagues or mentors can also help reinforce your confidence in your abilities.

- Seek Feedback Strategically: Identify individuals whose feedback you value and trust. Schedule regular check-ins or meetings with them to solicit constructive feedback on your work or performance. Prepare specific questions or areas of focus to guide the feedback discussion. Take notes during these sessions and use the feedback to identify areas for improvement and growth. Implementing feedback effectively demonstrates your commitment to continuous learning and development.

- Visualization Techniques: Set aside time each day for visualization exercises. Find a quiet and comfortable space where you can relax and focus your mind. Close your eyes and visualize yourself successfully accomplishing your goals or overcoming challenges. Engage all your senses by imagining the sights, sounds, and emotions associated with your desired outcomes. Incorporate positive affirmations into your visualization practice to reinforce your confidence and belief in your abilities. Regular visualization sessions can help build your confidence and mental resilience over time.

Step 3: Effective Communication Strategies

"Drowning in a sea of words, my voice struggles to navigate the currents of conversation,
lost in the vast expanse of extroverted expression."

In step 3 of your journey, let's delve into the realm of effective communication strategies tailored specifically for introverts. Recognizing that communication is a cornerstone of success in both professional and personal realms, let's explore how introverts can harness their unique strengths to communicate with impact and authenticity. This involves mastering not just the art of small talk and honing assertiveness but also embracing the critical role of non-verbal cues - from eye contact and body language to the subtleties of voice modulation, fundamental in conveying confidence, building connections, and enhancing the authenticity of your message. This step equips introverts with the tools and insights needed to thrive in diverse communication scenarios. Let's unlock the power of introvert-style communication and pave the way for greater confidence and influence in every interaction.

Overlapping speech bubbles represent the harmonization of listening and speaking in effective communication.

Why is effective communication critical for your success as an introvert?

The purpose of effective communication is to convey messages clearly, accurately, and persuasively in order to facilitate understanding, collaboration, and mutual respect among individuals or groups. Effective communication fosters meaningful connections, promotes positive relationships, and drives successful outcomes in personal, professional, and social contexts. It enables individuals to share information, express thoughts, and emotions, resolve conflicts, make informed decisions, and achieve common goals. Ultimately, the purpose of effective communication is to bridge gaps, build trust, and cultivate productive interactions that lead to shared understanding and mutual benefit.

Many times, you have a lot of great ideas, thoughts and views but hesitate to share them at the right time. Effective communication is crucial for introverts, empowering them to leverage their strengths, contribute meaningfully, and thrive in the workplace. By adopting introvert-style communication techniques, introverts can accelerate their professional development, foster strong relationships, and excel in diverse work environments. Additionally, honing these skills enables introverts to effectively navigate challenges and maximize their impact within their teams and organizations.

Harnessing the Power of Introvert-Style Communication

Let's delve into the art of harnessing the power of introvert-style communication. It's all about empowering introverted employees to accelerate their success by leveraging their unique strengths.

Introverts possess qualities that can contribute immensely to a team dynamic. They're deep thinkers, attentive listeners, and excellent observers. But often, they struggle to express themselves due to the dominance of extroverted communication styles. That's where this step comes in—it's all about providing introverted employees with valuable strategies to communicate effectively while staying true to themselves.

One crucial aspect of introvert-style communication is the art of active listening. Introverts excel in absorbing information and understanding others' perspectives. By actively listening, they can build strong relationships with colleagues and offer thoughtful solutions. It's all about practical techniques like maintaining eye contact, asking clarifying questions, and practicing reflective listening.

And then there's the power of written communication. Introverts often feel more comfortable expressing themselves through writing. By leveraging this strength and using platforms like email or project documentation, introverts can ensure their ideas are heard and valued. It's about crafting clear, concise, and persuasive written communication to make an impact.

Additionally, let's delve into the importance of finding your voice as an introvert. Many introverts struggle with self-confidence and fear of public speaking. But there are ways to overcome these challenges and empower yourself to speak up effectively. From mastering the art of storytelling to practicing assertive communication techniques, introverts can make their voices heard in meetings and presentations.

By harnessing the power of introvert-style communication, you can accelerate your success in the workplace. It's all about embracing your unique strengths, communicating effectively, and making a lasting impact. Whether you're an introvert looking to enhance your skills or an extrovert seeking to collaborate better with introverts, this step is a valuable resource for all. So why wait? Take the leap and unlock the hidden potential within you. After all, introverts have the power to thrive in any workplace environment.

Mastering the Art of Small Talk

Small talk has become an essential skill for success in the workplace. For introverted employees, who often find social interactions draining, small talk can be a daunting task. However, with a little guidance and practice, introverts can learn to excel in this art and leverage it to accelerate their success at work.

Small talk serves as the foundation for building relationships, networking, and creating opportunities. It may seem superficial, but it plays a crucial role in establishing rapport and opening doors for meaningful connections. By mastering the art of small talk, introverts can enhance their professional relationships, gain visibility, and create a positive impression among their colleagues and superiors.

> ### *Using Small Talk to warm up stakeholder meetings*
>
> *In preparation for meetings with stakeholders, I routinely engage in small talk to foster rapport and create a comfortable atmosphere. I ensure to have topics ready for discussion, ranging from the weather to recent weekend highlights, upcoming events, current organizational projects, local or national news, and sports.*
>
> *These topics provide a solid foundation for about 5 minutes of casual conversation, which typically amounts to around 10% of our meeting time. In a 45-minute meeting, dedicating 5 minutes to small talk helps establish a connection and cultivates warmth in the relationship. I make a conscious effort to avoid delving into personal matters, family discussions, or political topics. However, I may include family-related discussions if the individual has previously met my family or if there's a relevant context, such as someone's well-being.*

The first step in mastering small talk is to shift your mindset. Instead of viewing it as a tedious obligation, approach it as an opportunity to learn and connect with others. By reframing your perspective, you can alleviate the anxiety and actually enjoy the process. After all, small talk isn't about showcasing your knowledge—it's about showing genuine interest in others and making them feel valued.

Active listening is a vital skill that introverts naturally possess. Utilize this strength to your advantage during small talk conversations. Pay attention to the speaker's words, body language, and emotions. By listening actively and asking thoughtful questions, you can engage in deeper conversations and establish a meaningful connection.

It's always helpful to prepare some open-ended questions in advance to initiate conversations, don't you think? These questions can be about current events, shared interests, or industry-related topics. By having a few conversation starters ready, introverts can feel more confident and prepared to engage in small talk spontaneously.

Recognize the power of non-verbal communication. Introverts tend to be observant and thoughtful, so let's use this to our advantage. Maintain eye contact, have an open posture, and mirror the speaker's body language to establish trust and rapport. Non-verbal cues can convey your interest and attentiveness, making the conversation more enjoyable for both parties.

Lastly, don't forget to take breaks and recharge. As an introvert, social interactions can be draining. So, it's important to schedule short breaks between conversations to allow yourself some alone time to recharge and regain your energy. This way, you can sustain your engagement and make the most of every small talk opportunity.

By mastering the art of small talk, introverts can accelerate their success in the workplace. Embrace it as an opportunity to connect, learn, and grow. With practice and a positive mindset, introverted employees can excel in social interactions, enhance their professional relationships, and achieve their goals.

Quick exercise:

Prepare five sentences or questions you can use to initiate small talk with a stranger, whether it's a colleague or a participant you haven't met before, at a networking event.

1.

2.

3.

4.

5.

Here are a few examples:

- *"Hi there! Have you attended this event before, or is it your first time?"*
- *"What brings you to this networking event? Are you looking forward to any particular session?"*
- *"This venue is fantastic, isn't it? Have you been here before for other events?"*
- *"What's been the highlight of your day so far?"*
- *"I'm always curious to hear how people got started in their field. What's your origin story?"*
- *"I noticed you're from [mention their team or company]. What do you enjoy most about working there?"*

- *"Do you have any recommendations for other networking events or industry gatherings?"*
- *"How do you usually like to unwind after a busy week? Any favorite hobbies or activities?"*

Assertiveness Techniques for Introverts

The actions below aim to equip you with effective assertiveness techniques that will help you navigate professional settings with confidence and achieve your goals.

- Offer well-thought-out ideas and insights: Introverts have a natural ability to listen attentively, analyze situations deeply, and think critically. Recognize these strengths and use them to your advantage. By offering well-thought-out ideas and insights, you can assert yourself in a calm, intelligent manner.
- Prepare and practice: Before important meetings or discussions, take the time to prepare what you want to say. Create your own opinion or point of view about the topic. Write down your thoughts, key points, and questions. Practicing aloud can help you feel more confident and ensure that your message is clear and concise.
- Active listening: Engage in active listening by giving your full attention to the speaker. This not only shows respect but also allows you to gather valuable information. Take notes and ask thoughtful questions, which will not only demonstrate your assertiveness but also help you to contribute positively to the discussion.
- Use assertive body language: Body language plays a crucial role in assertiveness. Maintain eye contact, stand, or sit up straight, and use gestures to emphasize your points. This will convey confidence and ensure that your message is heard. *More on this topic at the end of this step.*

- Take small steps outside your comfort zone: Gradually challenge yourself to step outside your comfort zone. Volunteer for presentations or group projects, attend networking events or initiate conversations with colleagues. By stretching your boundaries, you will build confidence and assertiveness over time.

- Set boundaries: As an introvert, it's important to set boundaries to protect your energy and maintain a healthy work-life balance. Communicate your needs clearly and respectfully, whether it's requesting uninterrupted work time or declining after-work social events. Setting boundaries will help you maintain your productivity and prevent burnout.

Remember, assertiveness is not about being aggressive or dominating conversations. It is about expressing your thoughts, needs, and opinions in a confident and respectful manner. By embracing your introverted nature and utilizing these assertiveness techniques, you can accelerate your success at the workplace and showcase your invaluable contributions.

Actions for you to take:

- Understand your strengths:

  Action: Take time to reflect on your strengths as an introvert. Identify occasions where your listening skills or analytical thinking have proven valuable in past experiences. Acknowledge these strengths and consciously integrate them into your approach to work and interactions with others.

- Prepare and practice:

  Action: Develop a habit of preparing for important discussions by creating outlines or talking points. Practice articulating your ideas aloud, either alone or with a trusted colleague or mentor. This rehearsal will help refine your delivery and ease any nervousness.

- Active listening:

Action: Practice active listening techniques by focusing solely on the speaker during meetings or conversations. Avoid distractions and maintain eye contact to demonstrate your attentiveness. Take notes to capture key points and formulate thoughtful responses.

- Use assertive body language:

Action: Practice assertive body language techniques in front of a mirror or with a trusted friend or colleague. Experiment with standing tall, making deliberate gestures, and maintaining eye contact during conversations. Pay attention to how these cues influence perceptions of your confidence and authority.

Note: More details on non-verbal communication are at the end of this Step.

- Take small steps outside your comfort zone:

Action: Identify one specific area outside your comfort zone that you'd like to explore, such as public speaking or networking. Set achievable goals to engage in related activities, such as joining a public speaking club or attending a professional networking event. Celebrate each milestone as you stretch your limits and grow in confidence.

- Set boundaries:

Action: Take proactive steps to establish boundaries in your professional life by communicating your preferences and limitations to colleagues and supervisors. Practice assertive communication techniques to express your needs confidently and respectfully. Prioritize self-care and honor your boundaries to maintain optimal performance and fulfillment in your work.

Public Speaking and Presentations

Breaking Through: My Journey Overcoming Inhibitions

Once, someone asked me, "What am I afraid of?" While many people fear spiders, lizards, or cockroaches, my fear is dancing. With what felt like two left feet, the mere thought of being pulled onto a dance floor would send me running in the opposite direction. However, there came a moment when I found myself dancing in front of a crowd of thousands. It was during a Family Day event for all employees and families, where I was slated to perform on stage alongside a few colleagues. The key to overcoming my fear was preparation.

For an entire week leading up to the event, I dedicated myself to practice. I watched dance tutorials, mimicked the steps at home, and rehearsed tirelessly—each morning before going to work and every evening before bed. Gradually, I committed every move to memory until I felt entirely comfortable with the routine. When the day of the performance arrived, I found myself surprisingly eager for the act, realizing that performing was simply an extension of all the preparation I had invested.

This experience taught me a valuable lesson: thorough preparation can transform fear into eagerness. Whether it's delivering a speech, giving a presentation, or mastering a dance, readiness breeds confidence and enthusiasm for the task at hand.

Understanding Your Introvert Challenges

Public speaking and presentations pose unique challenges for introverts. The spotlight, the need for verbal expression on the spot, and the energy-draining nature of large gatherings can trigger anxiety. Addressing these challenges requires tailored strategies. Here are practical techniques for overcoming the anxiety of public speaking and presenting:

- **Preparation as a Confidence Booster**

  For you, thorough preparation is a cornerstone for overcoming anxiety in public speaking. Knowing the material inside out provides a safety net, reducing anxiety associated with potential uncertainties.

- **Structured Content and Clear Messaging**

  Structuring content and having a clear message help you maintain focus and coherence during presentations. This clarity enhances confidence as you navigate your narrative with precision.

To ensure audience engagement, consider integrating the following elements into your presentations:

✓ Structured Content: Organize your content logically, starting with identifying the problem, exploring potential solutions, presenting your recommendations, and providing reasons to support your suggestions. This structured approach keeps the audience focused and facilitates understanding.

✓ Establish Credibility: Demonstrate why the audience should value your insights and expertise. Also, establish why the topic you are speaking on is important for them, the WIIFM (what's in it for me). Highlight your qualifications, relevant experience, or unique perspective to establish credibility and build trust with your audience. Sometimes you can have someone do your introduction before you speak to establish this.

✓ Incorporate Facts and Data: Support your arguments with factual information and data-driven evidence. Incorporating statistics, research findings, or case studies adds credibility to your presentation and reinforces the validity of your recommendations.

✓ Utilize Infographics: Visual aids such as infographics help convey complex information in a visually appealing and digestible format. Use charts, graphs, or diagrams to illustrate key points and enhance audience comprehension.

✓ Include Compelling Images: Integrate relevant images that resonate with your audience and provide a human perspective to your content. Incorporating photographs or illustrations can evoke emotions, capture attention, and reinforce the narrative of your presentation.

✓ Allocate Time for Q&A: Reserve time at the end of your presentation for audience questions and discussion. Encouraging participation allows for clarification, engagement, and further exploration of topics raised during the presentation. Be prepared to address inquiries confidently and thoroughly to foster an interactive and informative session.

- **Utilizing Visual Aids**

  Visual aids serve as valuable tools for you during presentations. Whether it is slides, infographics, or charts, visual aids not only convey information effectively but also provide a focal point, easing the pressure on direct verbal communication.

  I have sometimes used an interesting picture, number, or an icon to remember and trigger the key points I would like to cover in the talk. If necessary, you should not hesitate to hold cue-cards to help you go through your presentation, especially if it is a long one.

- **Engaging in Gradual Exposure**

Gradually expose yourself to public speaking scenarios. Starting with smaller audiences or practicing in front of trusted individuals allows you to build confidence incrementally.

Begin by initiating conversations or sharing insights during team meetings, gradually expanding your involvement over time. You can proactively discuss with your reporting manager the possibility of contributing to weekly or monthly team meetings by sharing relevant updates or insights from your work. As you gain confidence, consider approaching the learning and development team to explore opportunities to lead brief training sessions or workshops on topics aligned with your expertise and interests. This gradual progression allows you to steadily build your public speaking skills while leveraging supportive environments within your organization.

- **Utilizing Pause and Reflection**

Embrace pauses during your presentations. These pauses not only allow for reflection but also create a sense of control, reducing anxiety and contributing to a more confident delivery.

Non-verbal Communication

Non-verbal cues play a pivotal role in effective communication, often speaking louder than words themselves. These silent signals, ranging from eye contact and facial expressions to body language and the subtleties of voice tone, form the unspoken backbone of our interactions. They have the power to convey authenticity, build trust, and create a deeper connection, transcending the limitations of verbal language. Understanding and mastering these non-verbal aspects of communication are essential for anyone looking to enhance their personal and professional relationships, making them indispensable tools for effective leadership and interpersonal engagement. In a world where words are plentiful, it's the unspoken nuances that truly shape our understanding and influence the impact of our message.

- **Eye Contact**: Maintaining appropriate eye contact signals confidence and establishes connections, showing engagement and interest. Actions:

  - Practice holding eye contact for a few seconds during conversations, gradually extending the duration to enhance comfort.
  - Employ the "triangle method," shifting your gaze between the other person's eyes and mouth for natural and comfortable eye contact.

- **Facial Expressions**: Conscious use of facial expressions conveys empathy, understanding, and attentiveness, effectively bridging communication gaps. Actions:

  - Practice expressive facial gestures in front of a mirror to better convey emotions like interest and happiness.
  - Remember to smile and nod during interactions to appear more engaged and approachable.

- **Body Language**: Open and inviting body language, such as uncrossed arms and an upright posture, signals openness and involvement. Actions:

  - Adopt an open stance by keeping arms relaxed at the sides or using them for natural gestures, avoiding crossed arms or legs.

- Practice maintaining good posture, standing, or sitting straight, to convey confidence.

- **Gestures**: Utilizing gestures can emphasize points and express enthusiasm, adding a layer of expressiveness to communication. Actions:

  - Incorporate hand movements to underline points when speaking, ensuring gestures are smooth and controlled.
  - Practice using open hand gestures to signify inclusivity and engagement.

- **Space and Proximity**: Being mindful of physical space and adjusting proximity according to the context influences the comfort level and dynamics of conversations. Actions:

  - Adjust your physical positioning based on the other person's body language to maintain engagement without encroaching on comfort zones.
  - Be aware of cultural norms regarding personal space in different settings, adapting, as necessary.

- **Listening Skills**: Active listening indicated through non-verbal cues like nodding and maintaining eye contact affirms the speaker and enhances rapport. Actions:

  - Show active listening by nodding in agreement, tilting your head, or giving verbal affirmations like "I see" to encourage the speaker.
  - Mirror the speaker's body language to subtly express empathy and foster a deeper connection.

- **Voice Tone and Pace**: The tone, pace, and volume of voice can significantly impact how a message is received, with modulation adding emphasis and clarity. Actions:

- Record yourself to become more aware of your tone and pace, then practice varying these elements to better convey different emotions.
- Implement breathing techniques to help control the volume and pitch, making your voice more impactful.

Actions for you to take:

Take proactive steps to enhance your non-verbal communication skills. Dedicate time each day, for at least a month, to activities like eye contact, facial expression, body language observation and adjustment, gesture refinement, spatial awareness reflection, active listening, and voice modulation exercises, each for 10-15 minutes. By focusing on these aspects and committing to improvement, you'll harness your innate ability for observation and reflection, transforming into a more impactful communicator and leader.

Speaking Without Words

In the first few months of my business development career, I found myself facing the daunting task of leading a critical meeting at work. As someone who naturally leans toward introversion, the idea of capturing and holding my colleagues' attention was nerve-racking. However, determined to turn this into a growth opportunity, I focused on refining my non-verbal communication skills, particularly eye contact and posture, which I believed could significantly enhance my presence and effectiveness without saying more words than necessary.

In the week leading up to the meeting, I set aside time each day to practice. Standing in front of my bedroom mirror, I rehearsed the main points of my presentation, paying close attention to maintaining steady eye contact with my reflection. Initially, it felt uncomfortable to hold my gaze even when the urge to look away was strong. But with each practice session, it became more natural. I employed the "triangle method," shifting my gaze gently between my reflection's eyes and mouth, imagining a triangle that helped distribute my attention evenly and avoid staring too intently.

Concurrently, I worked on my posture. I practiced standing with my feet firmly planted and my shoulders back, exuding a sense of confidence I didn't always feel. Whenever I caught myself slouching or folding my arms defensively during these practice sessions, I corrected my stance, reminding myself of the openness and authority good posture could convey. I remained conscious not to pace aimlessly, as if in a dance sequence, to avoid distracting the audience. Holding a marker/notepad in my hand also helped me manage any awkward gestures.

The day of the meeting arrived. I ensured I arrived at the venue a few minutes early to familiarize myself with the setting and comfortably greet attendees as they arrived. As I stood to present, I could feel the butterflies in my stomach. But as soon as I began, something remarkable happened. The practice paid off. My deliberate eye contact helped me connect with my audience, making the room feel smaller and more intimate. I noticed nods and smiles in return, signs of engagement I might have missed had I allowed my gaze to wander. My posture, too, seemed to silently broadcast a confidence that bolstered my words, making me feel anchored and in control.

The most telling moment came after the meeting when a colleague approached me. "You really had us all listening," they said. "It felt like you were talking to each of us personally." Their words were a testament to the power of those non-verbal cues I had worked so hard to incorporate.

This experience taught me that effective communication transcends words. As an introvert, I've always been comfortable in the realm of ideas and contemplation but learning to harness the power of non-verbal communication opened up new avenues for connection and influence. It was a vivid reminder that sometimes, how you say something can be as impactful as what you say, transforming not just how others perceive you but how you perceive yourself.

Summary:

Building self-confidence tailored to your introverted traits is a transformative journey. By recognizing and appreciating your unique strengths, you can navigate personal and professional challenges with increased assurance. The strategies and techniques discussed empower you to build confidence gradually, incorporating both verbal and non-verbal communication, setting the stage for success in various aspects of your life. In the realm of public speaking and presentations, understanding and addressing introvert-specific challenges pave the way for impactful and confident communication. Ultimately, the journey to building self-confidence for introverts is not about conforming to extroverted ideals but about embracing and amplifying the inherent strengths that make introverts invaluable contributors in their own distinctive way.

"With every word I speak, I compose a canvas of understanding, painting vivid portraits of ideas and emotions."

Step 4: Networking and Relationship Building

"Amidst the buzzing hive of social interaction, I feel like a solitary island, disconnected from the mainland of camaraderie and rapport."

Welcome to step 4 of your journey, where we delve into the intricacies of networking and relationship building tailored specifically for introverts. In this step, we explore a myriad of opportunities and strategies designed to align with your unique style and preferences. From intimate gatherings to larger networking events, you'll find practical advice and actionable tips to navigate socializing and mingling with confidence and authenticity. Let's unlock the secrets to forging meaningful connections and cultivating lasting relationships that propel you toward success in both professional and personal spheres.

A constellation of stars connected with each other symbolizing how introverts can form meaningful connections that create a supportive professional network.

Why are networking and building relationships important for introverts to be successful?

Networking and building relationships are crucial for you as an introvert to succeed, providing pathways for career advancement despite the challenges you may face in social settings. By leveraging your introverted strengths, you can forge meaningful connections that offer support, mentorship, and new opportunities.

While networking may not be your preferred activity due to the energy drain from large events and constant social interactions, it remains essential for your career growth. Fortunately, there are networking opportunities tailored to suit your introverted style, facilitating your success in the workplace.

Networking and Relationship Building Opportunities to Suit Your Style

Let's dive into the world of networking tailored specifically for introverted personalities, offering some practical tips to unlock success in the workplace.

Finding Networking Opportunities: When it comes to finding networking opportunities, it's all about playing to your strengths and preferences, right? Seek out smaller gatherings or industry-specific events where you can truly connect with others in a meaningful way. These settings provide the perfect backdrop for engaging in deeper conversations and forging genuine connections that align with your professional goals.

Leveraging Technology: Don't overlook the power of technology in expanding your network—it's a game-changer! Online platforms and social media offer a comfortable space for introverts to connect at their own pace. Take advantage of these digital tools to engage with like-minded professionals, share insights, and contribute to industry discussions—all from the comfort of your own environment.

Networking within the Organization: This is another goldmine for introverts. By participating in internal events, team building activities, and company workshops, you create opportunities to connect with colleagues and managers in familiar settings. These connections can lead to enhanced career growth and opportunities within the organization.

Nurturing Meaningful Connections: Remember, quality over quantity is important when it comes to nurturing connections. Invest your time in cultivating deep relationships and engaging in genuine conversations that build trust and rapport. By focusing on meaningful connections, you lay the foundation for a strong professional network that supports your long-term success.

Utilizing Social Media: Social media isn't just for sharing updates—it's a powerful tool for expanding your network globally. Engage in industry-specific online communities, participate in virtual conferences, and share your expertise through social platforms to make valuable contributions to your field.

Self-Promotion: Authentic self-promotion is key to gaining recognition and credibility in the workplace. Don't be shy about communicating your achievements and showcasing your strengths. By effectively promoting yourself, you establish yourself as a valuable contributor within your organization and industry.

Nurturing Professional Relationships: Don't forget the importance of demonstrating thoughtfulness in your interactions. Express appreciation in small, personalized ways and engage in genuine conversations to strengthen professional relationships. By showing thoughtfulness, you create a positive and supportive work environment conducive to your success.

In conclusion, networking and building relationships are vital for you to succeed in the workplace. By embracing your unique strengths, leveraging technology, and nurturing meaningful connections, you can unlock your full potential and thrive in your professional endeavors. With patience, persistence, and authenticity, you can navigate the social landscape with confidence and achieve your career goals.

Actions for you to take:

Networking and Building Relationships for Introverts:

- **Finding Networking Opportunities:**

    - Identify introverted strengths and preferences
    - Seek smaller, more intimate gatherings
    - Attend industry-specific conferences, workshops, or smaller networking groups
    - Look for events with a relaxed and casual atmosphere
    - Opt for settings conducive to deeper conversations and genuine connections

- **Leveraging Technology:**

    - Utilize online platforms and social media
    - Engage in industry-specific online communities
    - Participate in virtual conferences or webinars
    - Join professional networking platforms
    - Expand the network at your own pace in a comfortable environment

- **Networking Within the Organization:**

    - Participate in internal networking events
    - Attend team building activities

- Join company-sponsored workshops
- Connect with colleagues and managers
- Build relationships in familiar and smaller settings

- **Nurturing Meaningful Connections:**

  - Capitalize on active listening skills
  - Engage in genuine conversations
  - Focus on quality over quantity
  - Create a small circle of connections
  - Invest time in building deep relationships

- **Utilizing Social Media:**

  - Leverage technology to expand the network
  - Use online platforms for comfortable networking
  - Connect with like-minded professionals
  - Share expertise and insights
  - Make valuable contributions to industry discussions

- **Self-Promotion:**

  - Authentically communicate achievements and skills
  - Showcase unique strengths and contributions
  - Gain recognition and credibility in the workplace
  - Overcome discomfort with strategic self-promotion
  - Build visibility and reputation within professional circles

- **Nurturing Professional Relationships:**

  - Recognize and embrace introverted strengths
  - Establish trust and meaningful connections
  - Build a supportive network within the workplace
  - Focus on quality connections
  - Invest time and energy in cultivating deep relationships

- **Demonstrating Thoughtfulness:**

  - Use active listening skills to understand others' needs
  - Engage in genuine conversations
  - Show appreciation in small, personalized ways
  - Write handwritten notes or thoughtful emails
  - Express gratitude for colleagues' contributions

By leveraging these strategies, you can accelerate your success, excel in building lasting professional relationships, and thrive in a workplace that values your contributions while leveraging your thoughtful nature to nurture meaningful connections.

Practical Advice for Socializing and Mingling

Socializing and mingling, while seemingly second nature to extroverts, can be a nuanced art for introverts. However, with intentional approaches and practical advice, you can navigate social events, foster connections, and maintain a balance between social engagement and personal comfort.

✓ **Set Realistic Expectations:** Understand that socializing doesn't have to mean constant interaction. Set realistic expectations for yourself, allowing breaks for solitude to recharge when needed.

✓ **Identify Safe Conversation Starters:** Prepare a few safe and genuine conversation starters. This could range from discussing shared interests to asking about the other person's professional journey.

✓ **Create Exit Strategies:** Anticipate the need for breaks and create exit strategies for social situations that may become overwhelming. Politely excuse yourself for a breather when necessary.

✓ **Attend Smaller Gatherings:** Similar to networking, smaller gatherings provide a more comfortable setting for socializing. Focus on quality interactions, allowing for more meaningful connections.

✓ **Find Like-Minded Individuals:** Seek out individuals with similar interests or passions. Connecting over shared hobbies or topics can make social interactions more enjoyable and authentic.

✓ **Balance Social Engagement:** Strike a balance between social engagement and personal recharge time. It's perfectly acceptable to decline certain social invitations to prioritize self-care.

My journey through the networking Ballroom:

As I stepped into the grand ballroom, the vibrant hum of conversation enveloped me, setting my introverted heart aflutter. Socializing and mingling, while seemingly effortless for many, presented a nuanced challenge for me. Yet, armed with a few strategic tools, I ventured forth into the lively crowd, determined to navigate the evening with grace and authenticity.

The room was alive with laughter and chatter, a kaleidoscope of faces and voices swirling around me. I took a deep breath, steeling myself for the adventure ahead.

"Hey there! You look a bit lost," a friendly voice chimed in beside me. I turned to find Sarita, a colleague, flashing a warm smile.

"Yeah, I'm still trying to figure out my game plan for the evening," I admitted with a nervous chuckle.

Sarita nodded understandingly. "Tell you what, why don't we stick together? Strength in numbers, right?"

With a grateful smile, I accepted her offer, feeling a surge of relief wash over me. Together, we ventured into the heart of the crowd, weaving our way through clusters of animated conversation.

As the evening progressed, I found myself drawn into a lively discussion about travel with a group of fellow adventurers. Sharing stories of our most memorable journeys, I felt a sense of camaraderie and connection that buoyed my spirits.

But as the night wore on, the energy of the room began to take its toll. Sensing my growing unease, Sarita placed a comforting hand on my shoulder.

"Hey, how about we take a breather outside for a bit?" she suggested gently.

Gratefully, I nodded, relieved to escape the overwhelming cacophony of voices. Stepping out into the cool night air, I took a deep breath, savoring the quiet solitude.

Returning to the ballroom refreshed and rejuvenated, I found myself drawn to a smaller gathering in the corner. Engaging in intimate conversations and forging meaningful connections, I felt a sense of belonging that warmed my introverted soul.

As the night drew to a close, I couldn't help but marvel at how far I had come. Through moments of discomfort and uncertainty, I had discovered the strength and resilience within myself to thrive in the company of others. As I bid farewell to Sarita and the newfound friends I had made, I knew that this was just the beginning of my journey toward embracing my introverted nature and being more comfortable in any social setting.

Actions for You to Take:

Here are three interesting exercises for you to practice:

Coffee Shop Socializing Challenge:

- Choose a cozy, local coffee shop with a relaxed atmosphere.
- Set aside time to visit the coffee shop and engage in casual conversations with fellow patrons or friends.
- Challenge yourself to initiate conversations and build connections in this intimate setting.
- Tips:

  o Choose the Right Time: Pick a time when the coffee shop is not too crowded, allowing for more intimate conversations.
  o Start Small: Begin by making small talk with the staff or complimenting someone on their drink choice. These low-pressure interactions can help ease into longer conversations.

- Focus on Listening: Introverts excel at active listening, so focus on listening attentively to the responses of others. This can help build rapport and make the conversation more enjoyable.

Online Networking Adventure:

- Explore industry-specific online communities or forums that align with your interests.
- Participate in discussions, share insights, and connect with professionals in your field.
- Attend virtual conferences or webinars at your own pace, engaging with speakers and other attendees through online platforms.
- Tips:

    - Join Relevant Groups: Look for online communities or forums that align with your professional interests and goals. This ensures that your interactions are meaningful and valuable.
    - Share Insights: Contribute to discussions by sharing your expertise or asking thoughtful questions. This can help establish yourself as a knowledgeable and engaged member of the community.
    - Initiate Connections: Don't be afraid to reach out to other members privately to connect on shared interests or experiences. Personalized messages can lead to more meaningful connections.

Virtual Workshop Participation:

- Sign up for virtual workshops or training sessions offered by your company.
- Take advantage of these opportunities to connect with colleagues and managers in a more structured setting.

- Engage actively in group activities and discussions, fostering connections while learning new skills.
- Tips:

  o Prepare Ahead: Familiarize yourself with the workshop agenda and topics beforehand. This can help you feel more confident and prepared to contribute during discussions.

  o Participate Actively: Take advantage of opportunities to engage with the speaker and other attendees. Offer your insights, ask questions, and contribute to group activities to make the most of the workshop experience.

  o Follow Up: After the workshop, consider reaching out to participants you connected with to continue the conversation or exchange contact information. This can help solidify the connections you made during the event.

By engaging in these exercises, you can practice networking and relationship building in environments that cater to your preferences, ultimately enhancing your comfort and confidence in social interactions.

Ashwini's Journey of Strategic Self-Promotion

Ashwini had always been the invisible force behind her team's most successful projects at AuthenTech, a leading technology solutions company. As an introvert, she thrived in deep work and cherished her alone time for reflection and idea generation. However, Ashwini often felt overshadowed in a workplace that predominantly celebrated more vocal and extroverted traits.

On Monday morning, Ashwini arrived at work with a newfound resolve. She had spent the weekend reading about personal branding and strategic self-promotion and realized that to advance in her career, she needed to step out of her comfort zone and share her accomplishments more openly. She made a plan.

- ✓ ***Authentically Communicating Achievements:*** *Ashwini started by requesting a one-on-one meeting with her manager, Rashmi. During the meeting, she clearly communicated her recent achievements, detailing her role in the successful launch of the company's flagship product. She prepared a brief but impactful presentation that highlighted her contributions, emphasizing the skills she utilized to navigate and solve critical challenges throughout the project. She also started maintaining a brag sheet thereafter.*

- ✓ ***Showcasing Unique Strengths:*** *In team meetings, Ashwini began to actively share insights and solutions that showcased her unique strengths. She took the lead in explaining the technical complexities of current projects, offering detailed explanations that only she, with her deep understanding, could provide. Her colleagues quickly began to see her as a go-to expert in solving complex software issues.*

- ✓ ***Gaining Recognition and Credibility:*** *To build her credibility, Ashwini contributed articles to the company newsletter, sharing tips on software development best practices. She also volunteered to conduct a workshop on code optimization techniques. Her initiatives were well-received, earning her praise not just from her immediate team but from senior management as well.*

- ✓ ***Overcoming Discomfort with Self-Promotion:*** *The biggest challenge for Ashwini was overcoming her discomfort with self-promotion. She tackled this by setting small, achievable goals for sharing her work. She started discussions on the company's internal social media platform, gradually increasing her visibility among peers across the company. Each positive interaction boosted her confidence.*

- ✓ ***Building Visibility and Reputation:*** *Realizing the power of professional networking, Ashwini updated her LinkedIn profile, highlighting her key projects and skills. She joined several* *professional groups online and began engaging with content relevant to her field. Soon, she found herself at ease, discussing industry trends with professionals worldwide, which enhanced her reputation both inside and outside the company.*

As the months passed, Ashwini's strategic efforts to promote herself paid off. She was not only nominated for the "Innovator of the Year" award at AuthenTech but also invited to speak at a regional conference on technology. Through her journey, Ashwini transformed her workplace presence, aligning her introverted nature with a proactive approach to career advancement.

Ashwini's story is a testament to the fact that even the least visible individuals can make a significant impact by authentically promoting their achievements and capabilities. In doing so, they not only advance their own careers but also enrich their workplaces with their unique perspectives and skills.

Summary:

Navigating the social landscape as an introvert requires embracing your unique strengths and approaching interactions with authenticity. By implementing effective networking strategies and practical advice for socializing, you can build meaningful connections and thrive in both professional and social settings. Remember, the key is not to conform to extroverted norms but to leverage your introverted qualities in creating genuine and valuable relationships.

"Amidst the sea of faces, I navigate with purpose,
forging connections that bloom into alliances, anchored in trust and
reciprocity."

Step 5: Excelling in Teamwork and Collaboration

"As the gears of collaboration grind, I find myself caught in the cogs, struggling to synchronize my introverted rhythm with the extroverted symphony."

Welcome to step 5 of your journey, where we explore the dynamic realm of teamwork and collaboration through the lens of introverted strengths. In this step, we delve into the nuances of leveraging your unique attributes to thrive in team settings, fostering effective communication strategies that resonate with introverted tendencies. From navigating group dynamics to overcoming challenges in collaborative projects, we provide insights and practical techniques to excel in collective endeavors while staying true to your introverted nature. Let's unravel the secrets to unlocking the full potential of introverted individuals within team environments, forging pathways to success through synergy and cooperation.

A puzzle with a few pieces coming together to complete the picture, highlighting the value of collaboration and how each unique piece/person is vital to the whole.

Why is it important for Introverts to excel in teamwork and collaboration?

Excelling in teamwork and collaboration is crucial for introverts in their careers because it offers opportunities to gain diverse perspectives, enhance communication skills, foster professional growth, access networking opportunities, contribute to team success, and align with organizational values, ultimately leading to career advancement and fulfillment.

What's the challenge? As an introvert, you may often face unique challenges when working in teams and collaborating, primarily due to common misconceptions about introversion and the typically extroverted structures of many workplaces. Since you generally prefer solitude, you might experience overstimulation in noisy or chaotic team environments, and the limited quiet time available in such settings can make it difficult for you to find the necessary breaks to recharge. Additionally, you may often feel pressure to conform to frequent meetings and collaborative sessions, which can be draining. Furthermore, your preference for written communication over verbal exchanges is not always valued equally in collaborative settings.

What needs to be done? So, let's tackle these unique challenges head-on with some targeted strategies. First up, don't be afraid to communicate your preferred work style to your teammates and managers. Educating them about what conditions help you perform best can make a world of difference. Plus, it shows that you're proactive about creating an environment where everyone can thrive.

Now, let's talk visibility. It's all about finding strategic ways to enhance your presence. Whether it's volunteering for a public speaking opportunity or adapting your style to fit different situations, there are plenty of ways to shine without stepping too far out of your comfort zone.

And let's not forget about your strengths. As an introvert, you bring a unique perspective to the table. From your active listening skills to your knack for strategic problem-solving, you've got a lot to offer that can really enrich team dynamics and boost productivity.

These strategies are all about empowering you to navigate teamwork and collaboration with confidence. By building strong one-on-one relationships and playing to your strengths, you'll not only improve overall teamwork but also make those group settings a little less daunting.

So, introverts, let's embrace our strengths and show the world what we're made of. You can foster a culture of inclusivity and innovation that benefits everyone in the workplace.

- **Effective Team Communication Strategies:**

  - Combine active listening techniques, thoughtful contributions, and balancing social engagement under one umbrella to emphasize your comprehensive communication skills.
  - Engage in attentive listening, prepare your thoughts in advance, and use breaks strategically to recharge and maintain productivity.

- **Building Meaningful Connections:**

  - Integrate building one-on-one relationships and strategic collaboration. Focus on the importance of deep, authentic connections and how they improve teamwork and comfort in your group settings.
  - Seek opportunities for smaller group interactions or one-on-one collaborations to foster deeper connections.

- **Enhance Your Visibility Strategically:**

  - Document your contributions and engage selectively, ensuring your participation aligns with your strengths and offers maximum impact.

  - Emphasize achieving strategic visibility through regular updates and selective engagement in meetings and projects.

- **Embrace and Communicate Your Work Style:**

  - Advocate for your needs by educating others about your work style, such as your preference for written communication and the need for quiet time.

  - Structure your environment by creating quiet spaces and scheduling downtime, which is essential for managing overstimulation and maintaining productivity.

- **Leveraging Your Strengths in Team Settings:**

  - Focus on how your natural tendencies like active listening, observing, and strategic problem-solving can be leveraged to add value in team settings.

  - Play to your strengths, such as deep analytical thinking and strategic planning, especially in roles that require intensive thought and independent work.

  - Offer innovative solutions that consider all angles, driving the team toward effective resolutions.

- **Expand Your Skills:**

  - Stress on continuous learning and adaptation, such as engaging in public speaking and flexibly adapting your style when needed.

- Practice public speaking in safe environments and learn to stretch your comfort zone to better fit dynamic workplace demands.

In the area of teamwork and collaboration, you play a pivotal role in fostering innovation, empathy, and inclusivity. By embracing your unique strengths and adopting tailored strategies for effective communication and collaboration, you unlock your full potential as a catalyst for organizational success. As workplaces strive to cultivate environments that celebrate diversity and harness individual talents, empowering introverts becomes not just a strategic imperative but a testament to the transformative power of inclusive teamwork.

Self-reflection Exercise:

Key Anxieties for Introverts in Teamwork and Collaboration:

1. Fear of Speaking Up: Introverts may feel anxious about speaking up in group settings, fearing judgment or rejection from their peers.
2. Overwhelm in Large Groups: Introverts may feel overwhelmed or drained in large group settings, where there are many voices and competing ideas.
3. Difficulty Building Relationships: Introverts may struggle to build relationships with team members, particularly in fast-paced or high-pressure environments.

Self-Reflection Questions:

By reflecting on these key anxieties and asking yourself these self-reflection questions, you can gain deeper insights into your challenges with teamwork and collaboration as an introvert. This self-awareness can empower you to develop strategies to overcome these anxieties, build more meaningful relationships with your team members, and thrive in collaborative environments.

Fear of Speaking Up:

- Have there been instances where I hesitated to share my ideas or opinions in team meetings? What thoughts or emotions were present during those moments?
- What strategies can I implement to overcome my fear of speaking up and contribute more confidently to group settings?
- How can I remind myself of the value that my unique perspective brings to team discussions?

Overwhelm in Large Groups:

- How do I typically feel in large group meetings or brainstorming sessions? What specific triggers contribute to my feelings of overwhelm?
- What coping mechanisms have I used in the past to manage overwhelm in large group settings? How effective were these strategies?
- Are there ways I can proactively create a more comfortable environment for myself in large group situations, such as sitting in a specific location or taking breaks as needed?

Difficulty Building Relationships:

- Do I find it challenging to initiate conversations or build rapport with my team members? What barriers or obstacles do I encounter in forming relationships?
- Are there common interests or shared experiences that I can leverage to connect with my colleagues on a deeper level?
- How can I prioritize building relationships with key team members to foster trust and collaboration within the team?

Govind's Story of Collaboration

Govind, with his introverted disposition, often felt like a solitary island amidst a sea of extroverted energy. As he navigated the intricacies of teamwork and collaboration, he found himself grappling with the relentless tide of group dynamics and interpersonal interactions.

One fateful day, Govind found himself thrust into a high-stakes project that demanded extensive collaboration across departments. As he entered the boardroom for the kick-off meeting, he could feel the weight of anticipation hanging heavy in the air.

"Govind, glad you could join us," greeted his colleague, Madhu, with a warm smile. Madhu was known for her outgoing nature and effortless charm, a stark contrast to Govind's reserved demeanor.

"Thanks, Madhu," replied Govind, mustering a polite smile in return. Despite his best efforts to mask his unease, he couldn't shake the nagging feeling of apprehension gnawing at his insides.

As the meeting progressed, Govind found himself struggling to assert himself amidst the cacophony of voices vying for attention. With each passing minute, his anxiety mounted, threatening to engulf him in a suffocating wave of self-doubt.

"Hari, what are your thoughts on the project timeline?" Madhu's voice cut through the din, redirecting the spotlight to Govind's colleague seated across from him.

Hari, a confident and articulate team lead, launched into a detailed analysis of the project milestones, effortlessly commanding the room with his authoritative presence.

Watching Hari effortlessly navigate the complexities of group dynamics, Govind couldn't help but feel a pang of envy. Why couldn't he possess the same innate ability to command attention and respect?

Determined to break free from the shackles of self-doubt, Govind embarked on a journey of self-discovery and growth. Armed with actionable strategies, he set out to harness his introverted strengths and carve a path to success on his own terms.

Instead of allowing his reservations to hold him back, Govind made a conscious effort to actively listen and observe during team meetings. He focused on absorbing information deeply before formulating his thoughts, allowing him to contribute valuable insights that often went unnoticed by his more vocal colleagues.

When it came to communication, Govind adopted a strategic approach, preparing his thoughts in advance and leveraging written communication channels to articulate his ideas effectively. He ensured that his contributions were well-thought-out and impactful, emphasizing quality over quantity.

Rather than allowing himself to become overwhelmed in large group settings, Govind prioritized self-care and set boundaries to maintain a healthy balance between social engagement and personal recharge time. He scheduled regular breaks to gather his thoughts and recharge, ensuring optimal productivity during team interactions.

As the project progressed, Govind found himself navigating the challenges of group projects with newfound grace and resilience. With each passing day, he grew more confident in his abilities, harnessing the power of his introverted strengths to excel in teamwork and collaboration.

In the end, Govind emerged triumphant, a light of inspiration for introverts everywhere. Through sheer determination and unwavering perseverance, he had shattered the barriers that once held him back, paving the way for a future filled with limitless possibilities.

How good are you with Teamwork and Collaboration Skills?

Self-assessment

Take this self-assessment. Rate each of the statements on a scale of 1 to 5. Please choose the number that best represents your feelings, thoughts, and behaviors.

Less True 1   2   3   4   5 More True

S.No.	Statement	Your response
1	I effectively communicate my ideas and opinions in team settings, contributing to group discussions.	
2	I work well with others, recognizing and valuing diverse perspectives within the team.	
3	I actively seek opportunities to collaborate with team members, recognizing the value of teamwork in achieving goals.	
4	I effectively manage conflicts within the team, seeking mutually beneficial resolutions.	
5	I adapt my communication style to fit the preferences of different team members, ensuring effective communication.	
6	I actively participate in team meetings and collaborative activities, contributing to the team's success.	

S.No.	Statement	Your response
7	I take initiative in identifying and addressing team challenges, working collaboratively to find solutions.	
8	I build strong relationships with team members, fostering a positive and supportive team environment.	
9	I actively seek feedback from team members to improve my teamwork and collaboration skills.	
10	I effectively delegate tasks and responsibilities within the team, leveraging each member's strengths.	

Scoring: Please add up all 'Your responses' and review your score in the Score Key.

Score Key

Score Interpretation: Here's what your score might indicate:

- Total Score 40-50: Excellent Team Player: You demonstrate exceptional teamwork and collaboration skills. Your ability to communicate effectively, work well with others, and adapt to different team dynamics is commendable.

- Total Score 30-39: Good Team Player: You have strong teamwork and collaboration skills but may benefit from further development in some areas. Consider seeking feedback and actively working on areas of improvement.

- Total Score 20-29: Room for Improvement: There is room for improvement in your teamwork and collaboration skills. Focus on enhancing your communication, conflict resolution, and adaptability to become a more effective team player.

- Total Score 10-19: Needs Improvement: Your teamwork and collaboration skills may be hindering team effectiveness. Consider seeking feedback, training, or mentorship to improve your skills in these areas.

"In the symphony of collaboration, my voice harmonizes with others, each note is resonating with synergy and innovation."

Step 6: Strategies for Introvert Leadership

"Balancing on the tightrope of leadership, I tread cautiously, mindful of the chasm below, where the expectations of extroversion threaten to engulf my introspective nature."

Welcome to step 6 of your journey, where we embark on a transformative exploration of leadership tailored to introverted strengths. In this step, we delve deep into the intricate aspects of introverted leadership, guiding you through a holistic journey of self-discovery, empowerment, and growth. By embracing your introverted nature as a source of power rather than limitation, we uncover the essence of authentic leadership. From cultivating your unique leadership style to prioritizing self-care and fostering continuous growth, we provide a comprehensive roadmap for aspiring introverted leaders. Drawing inspiration from stories of introverted leaders from India and beyond, we illuminate the path to leading with confidence, compassion, and unwavering authenticity. Let's navigate the terrain of introverted leadership, harnessing the transformative potential to inspire and empower others on the journey to success.

A queen standing out from others on the chess board symbolizing strategic thinking and leadership, emphasizing the introvert's ability to lead with thoughtfulness and insight.

Why do you need to consider putting in extra effort?

Navigating the professional world as an introvert presents unique challenges, especially when aiming for leadership roles. The prevailing notion favoring extroverts in leadership can be disheartening. However, recognizing and embracing your distinct strengths is crucial. You, as an introverted leader, often face obstacles related to communication, networking, and assertiveness—qualities typically prized in leadership. Additionally, you must combat stereotypes and misconceptions about introversion's compatibility with leadership. As a result, you may need to invest extra effort to surmount these barriers.

By dedicating yourself to areas like relationship building, effective communication, and stepping out of your comfort zone, you can demonstrate your capabilities and attain success in leadership roles. With actionable strategies and practical advice, you can empower yourself to excel and thrive in leadership positions.

The Silent Exodus: An Introvert's Fall in the Merger Maze

In the dim light of the early hours, Vikram Mehta, the COO of GreenwoodTech Financial, sat in his office surrounded by ledgers and projections. A man of few words, his leadership style was one of action and introspection. Under his guidance, GreenwoodTech had weathered storms and emerged resilient, yet today, he faced a tempest unlike any other—the impending merger with HighTower Capital.

Vikram had always been at odds with the culture at HighTower, a firm where charisma often trumped capability, and visibility was synonymous with value. He knew the merger was not just a blending of assets but of cultures, and in this new world, his quiet leadership was at risk.

As D-day approached, Vikram met with Sharat Khanna, the CEO of HighTower, in a high-stakes meeting to discuss the integration plan.

Sharat, with his magnetic presence and booming voice, was the antithesis of Vikram.

"Vikram, you've built a fine ship here at GreenwoodTech," Sharat began, his voice echoing in the spacious boardroom. "But to navigate the waters ahead, we'll need more than a steady hand. We need a voice that commands the room, rallies the troops, and mesmerizes customers. You understand, don't you?"

Vikram nodded, his apprehension growing. "I believe leadership isn't just about being heard," he said quietly. "It's about listening, understanding, and then guiding. It's what's brought us this far."

Sharat laughed heartily. "Ah, but we're playing in the big leagues now, Vikram. It's about bold moves, about being at the forefront. It's a different game."

The merger went through, and the integration began. Offices merged, departments blended, and amidst this, Vikram found himself increasingly side-lined. Meetings were held without his input, and decisions were made without his counsel. His once-valued silence, which had been a space for thought and strategy, was now seen as hesitance, a lack of initiative.

Whispers filled the corridors, and soon enough, Vikram was called into what would be his final meeting with Sharat and the newly formed board.

"Vikram, we appreciate everything you've done," Sharat started, his voice unusually subdued. "But we believe it's time for new leadership to steer GreenwoodTech in this new chapter. Someone more... aligned with our vision."

The words struck Vikram not as a surprise but as the inevitable conclusion to a narrative he had seen unfold. The quiet leader, once at the helm of GreenwoodTech's success, was now an outlier in the boisterous world of HighTower's.

As Vikram packed his office, his life's work condensed into a box of personal items; he paused at the framed picture of GreenwoodTech's founding team. A team that had believed in him, in his vision, and in his quiet strength.

Leaving the keys on his desk, Vikram walked out of the building for the last time, the setting sun casting long shadows. The corridors that had once echoed with his silent commands now whispered the tale of the introverted leader who, in the end, was silenced not by failure but by a world that couldn't hear his wisdom.

Commentary: *Many introverted senior leaders encounter situations like what Vikram Mehta faced, particularly when there's a significant shift at the helm due to new leadership stepping in or through mergers and acquisitions. Such transitions often bring to the forefront a clash of cultures where the innate strengths of introverted leaders may not be immediately apparent to new leadership. In the hustle of reorganization and the rush to align with the new vision, the quiet, strategic contributions of introverts often go unnoticed, leaving scant time for their value to be recognized and understood. This lack of visibility, coupled with a limited window to bridge understanding, can, unfortunately, lead to talented leaders being side-lined, their potential contributions untapped in a rush toward transformation. Could Vikram have done something to change this trajectory?*

Distinctive Leadership Capabilities

In the realm of effective leadership, four distinct capabilities emerge as pivotal for catalyzing success and nurturing organizational growth: the Brand Driver, Strategic Delivery, Collaborative Catalyst, and Innovative Integrator. These capabilities serve as the foundational pillars of leadership, encompassing everything from the cultivation of a robust brand reputation to the strategic navigation of the organization toward its objectives. Leaders are tasked not only with inspiring and rallying their teams toward shared success but also with fostering innovation and the fluid integration of new ideas into the organizational ethos. By mastering these capabilities, leaders are equipped to adeptly maneuver through the complexities of today's dynamic business environment, ensuring their teams and organizations do not just endure but flourish amidst continuous change.

- **Brand Driver**: Embodying the essence of leading by example, Brand Drivers build a robust personal and organizational reputation while ensuring the translation of vision into actionable outcomes. They inspire trust and command respect, seamlessly turning strategic plans into tangible successes that underscore the brand's value and integrity.

- **Strategic Delivery**: Specialists in Strategic Delivery craft and communicate visionary paths forward, making informed decisions that propel the organization toward growth. By setting ambitious yet achievable goals, they navigate the organization through complexities, delivering significant value and enhancing stakeholder confidence through strategic foresight and execution.

- **Collaborative Catalyst**: As a nexus of persuasion and inspiration, Collaborative Catalysts foster a culture where collaboration thrives, and synergy is the norm. By rallying teams around shared goals and leveraging diverse strengths, they enhance collective outcomes, creating an environment where mutual support and effective influence lead to innovative solutions and organizational success.

- **Innovative Integrator**: At the forefront of change, Innovative Integrators foster an environment ripe for creativity and continuous improvement. By championing innovation and investing in team development, they ensure the organization remains competitive and adaptable. Their leadership not only sparks pioneering ideas but also weaves these innovations into the fabric of the organization, investing in developing the skills and talents of their teams and building capabilities that sustain long-term growth and evolution.

While introverts bring unique strengths to leadership, certain aspects of the four capabilities might not come as naturally to them, requiring deliberate effort to enhance their effectiveness in these areas:

- **Brand Driver**: Introverts may find the public aspects of building a personal and organizational reputation challenging, as it often requires a high-level of visibility and engagement with a wide audience. They might need to work on comfortably promoting their achievements and the organization's successes in more public forums.

- **Strategic Delivery**: While introverts are often strong in strategic thinking due to their reflective nature, the challenge may lie in assertively communicating their vision and ensuring it mobilizes the organization. Developing persuasive communication skills and confidently articulating their strategies to a broader audience can be areas for growth.

- **Collaborative Catalyst**: Introverts naturally excel at deep, one-on-one connections, but they might find it more challenging to foster collaboration and synergy in larger group settings. Working on facilitating open communication and actively engaging in team dynamics can help introverts become more effective in harnessing collective strengths.

- **Innovative Integrator**: Introverts are often innovative thinkers, but they may struggle with integrating these innovations across the organization due to a potential hesitation to advocate for their ideas assertively. Enhancing their ability to champion new initiatives and rallying support from a diverse group of stakeholders can be crucial for their success in this area.

For introverts to remain successful in these leadership capabilities, focusing on developing skills in public speaking, assertive communication, team facilitation, and stakeholder engagement can be highly beneficial. Leveraging their natural strengths, such as thoughtful reflection and a focus on deep connections, can also aid in overcoming these challenges.

Embracing Your Introverted Nature

Before diving into leadership strategies, it's crucial to understand and celebrate your introverted traits. By recognizing the inherent value in qualities such as deep thinking, active listening, and empathy, you can cultivate confidence and harness these strengths to lead effectively.

Action Points:

- Reflect on your introverted strengths and how they contribute to your leadership style.
- Embrace your natural tendencies, such as thoughtful reflection and empathy, as assets in leadership roles.
- Seek out examples of successful introverted leaders for inspiration and validation.

Discovering Your Leadership Style

Every leader has a unique style, and as an introvert, it's important to find an approach that aligns with your natural tendencies. By focusing on qualities like thoughtfulness, empathy, and strategic thinking, you can lead authentically and earn the respect of your team.

Action Points:

- Reflect on your values and leadership philosophy to define your personal leadership style.
- Identify key strengths and areas for growth and develop strategies to leverage them effectively.
- Seek feedback from colleagues and mentors to refine your leadership approach and communication style.

Cultivating a Strong Network

Building a strong network is essential for leadership growth. However, introverts may prefer meaningful one-on-one or small group connections over large social gatherings. By engaging in deeper conversations and establishing genuine connections, you can create a supportive network of mentors, collaborators, and peers.

Action Points:

- Identify individuals within your organization or industry whose values align with yours and initiate conversations to build relationships.
- Engage with senior leaders to enhance your visibility and establish your presence as a leader.
- Attend smaller networking events or seek out opportunities for one-on-one meetings to connect with like-minded professionals.
- Offer support and assistance to others in your network, fostering reciprocity and trust.

Prioritizing Self-Care

Leadership roles can be draining for introverts, so prioritizing self-care is essential. Taking regular breaks, setting boundaries, and engaging in activities that replenish your energy are crucial for maintaining effectiveness as a leader while preserving your mental and emotional well-being.

Action Points:

- Establish boundaries around your time and energy and communicate them clearly to colleagues and team members.
- Schedule regular breaks throughout the day to recharge and reflect.
- Engage in activities that promote relaxation and well-being, such as meditation, exercise, or hobbies.

Pursuing Continuous Growth

The journey to leadership is a continuous one, and introverts can accelerate their growth by seeking out opportunities for professional development. Whether through workshops, courses, or coaching programs, investing in your skills and knowledge is key to staying ahead of the curve.

Role of Coaching for Career Success:

- Coaching can help introverts identify weaknesses and leverage strengths.
- Develop strategies for clear communication and assertiveness.
- Gain guidance on using strengths to advantage and building confidence.

Action Points:

- Identify areas for growth and development in your leadership skills and seek out relevant training or resources.
- Actively seek feedback from colleagues, mentors, and supervisors to identify strengths and areas for improvement.
- Set goals for your professional development and create a plan to achieve them, including timelines and milestones.

Leading Meetings and Presentations with Confidence

Effective communication is a cornerstone of leadership, and introverts can excel in leading meetings and presentations with the right strategies. By preparing effectively, utilizing introverted strengths like active listening, and embracing relaxation techniques, you can confidently lead discussions and presentations, inspiring trust, and confidence in your team.

Action Points:

- Prepare thoroughly for meetings and presentations, including researching the topic, organizing your thoughts, and anticipating questions.
- Practice active listening during meetings, allowing others to contribute their ideas and perspectives.
- Utilize relaxation techniques, such as deep breathing or visualization, to calm nerves before speaking in public.

Throughout my leadership journey, I've been privileged to address large gatherings on numerous significant occasions—be it celebrating milestones, launching new initiatives, or leading strategic meetings. Each time I stood before the crowd, I adhered to three cardinal rules that not only honed my speeches but ensured they resonated deeply with my audience.

Firstly, I meticulously distilled my message into three core points. These were the pillars of my speech: crucial, memorable, and impactful. They were not just easy for me to recall amid the nerves and spotlight but were crafted to leave a lasting impression on my listeners.

Secondly, I consistently focused on the audience's perspective. "What's in it for them?" was the question at the heart of my preparation. I delved into why they should care about the subject, what they needed to understand,

and, importantly, how the discussed matter directly influenced their lives or work. This approach helped in making my message relevant and engaging.

Finally, I ensured that every speech was a two-way conversation. I invited questions, encouraged dialogue, and welcomed their concerns. This engagement was not merely about interaction but about building a connection, making each session a collaborative and dynamic exchange rather than a monologue.

These principles guided me through countless addresses, each a story of shared thoughts and mutual growth—a testament to the power of communication in leadership.

Building and Inspiring High-Performing Teams

Building and inspiring high-performing teams requires a combination of introverted qualities and leadership skills. By fostering thoughtful discussions, connecting with like-minded colleagues, advocating for uninterrupted time, encouraging diverse perspectives, and leading by example, introverted leaders can create environments where all team members can thrive and excel.

Action Points:

- Foster an inclusive and collaborative team culture by encouraging open communication and valuing diverse perspectives.
- Connect with like-minded colleagues to build relationships based on shared values and working styles.
- Lead by example by demonstrating dedication, integrity, and a commitment to excellence in your own work.

As an introverted leader, you have the power to make a significant impact in your organization. By recognizing and embracing your unique strengths, cultivating a supportive network, prioritizing self-care, pursuing continuous growth, and leading with confidence and authenticity, you can unlock your leadership potential and accelerate your success in the workplace. It's time to celebrate the power of introversion and harness it to drive positive change and achieve success in your leadership journey.

Amplifying Introverted Leadership: A Self-Assessment for Recognition and Growth

Please rate how often you engage in the following actions in your leadership role, using a scale from 1 to 5:

1 - Rarely or Never 2 - Occasionally 3 - Sometimes 4 - Often 5 - Always or Almost Always

S.No.	Statement	Your response
1	I actively seek opportunities to share and celebrate my achievements and those of my team in public settings, even when it feels outside my comfort zone.	
2	I have strategies in place to enhance my visibility and the visibility of my organization's successes, utilizing platforms and forums that align with my strengths.	
3	I utilize digital and social media platforms effectively to build and communicate my personal and organizational brand, adapting my approach to suit these public channels.	
4	I regularly engage in networking events and professional gatherings, intentionally promoting our achievements to broaden our reach and impact.	

S.No.	Statement	Your response
5	I confidently communicate my strategic vision to a wide audience, ensuring my ideas mobilize the organization toward our common goals.	
6	I continuously work on refining my communication skills to be more persuasive and impactful when articulating strategies.	
7	I ensure my strategic plans are not only well thought out but also clearly documented and accessible, facilitating easier communication and buy-in from my team and stakeholders.	
8	I seek feedback on my vision and strategy from diverse perspectives within the organization to refine and strengthen my approach to strategic delivery.	
9	I take proactive steps to foster collaboration and synergy within my team, facilitating open communication to ensure all voices are heard.	
10	I actively engage in larger group dynamics, working to create an environment where collective strengths are harnessed and celebrated.	
11	I initiate and participate in cross-functional projects to foster broader collaboration and understand the diverse dynamics within my organization.	
12	I provide platforms and opportunities for my team members to lead collaborative efforts, promoting a culture of shared leadership and mutual support.	

S.No.	Statement	Your response
13	I advocate for my innovative ideas with conviction, ensuring they gain the visibility and support needed to be integrated across the organization.	
14	I seek out and engage diverse groups of stakeholders to rally support for new initiatives, overcoming any hesitation to put my ideas forward.	
15	I conduct regular brainstorming sessions with teams across the organization to gather a wide range of ideas, demonstrating openness and advocacy for innovation.	
16	I create and maintain a process for evaluating and implementing innovative ideas, ensuring they are aligned with our strategic objectives and have the necessary support to succeed.	

Score Interpretation:

- 61 - 80: Exceptional Leadership! Your score indicates a strong engagement with proactive strategies that elevate your leadership while embracing your introverted qualities. You're effectively managing visibility challenges, advocating for your ideas, and fostering collaboration. Your efforts to ensure your contributions are recognized set a benchmark for leadership growth.

- 41 - 60: Promising Potential! This scoring range shows you're leveraging your introverted strengths and addressing the challenges of visibility and recognition with a proactive stance. You've started to navigate the balance between introversion and outward leadership expression, suggesting room for further growth in making your leadership acknowledged and valued more broadly.

- 25 - 40: Developing Awareness! Your responses suggest an emerging awareness of the importance of balancing introverted qualities with proactive visibility measures. By focusing on strategies to highlight your leadership, such as engaging in networking and advocating for your strategies and innovations, you can greatly enhance your effectiveness and recognition.

- 16 - 24: Foundation for Growth! At this foundational level, there's a crucial opportunity to further develop your leadership qualities by adopting strategies that increase your visibility and mitigate the risk of being overlooked. Concentrating on enhancing your public engagement, strategic communication, and collaborative initiatives is essential for advancing your performance and recognition as a leader.

Actions for you to take:

Embracing Introverted Leadership Qualities

- **Deep Listening:** Introverts excel in active listening, absorbing information thoughtfully. Use this strength to understand your team's perspectives, foster collaboration, and make well-informed decisions.

- **Thoughtful Decision-Making:** The introspective nature of introverts lends itself to careful and deliberate decision-making. Embrace this quality to navigate complex situations, considering various angles before arriving at well-thought-out conclusions.

- **Empathy and Understanding:** Introverts often possess a heightened sense of empathy. Leverage this quality to connect with team members on a deeper level, creating a supportive and understanding work environment.

- **Focus on Individual Contributions:** Recognize and appreciate individual contributions within the team. Introverted leaders can excel in acknowledging the unique strengths of each team member, fostering a sense of value, and belonging.

- **Leading by Example:** Introverted leaders can inspire by leading through actions. Demonstrate commitment, dedication, and a strong work ethic to set a positive example for the team.

Navigating Challenges as an Introverted Leader

- **Balancing Communication Styles:** Acknowledge the need for effective communication while respecting your preference for thoughtful expression. Find a balance that ensures clear communication without compromising your authentic communication style.

- **Delegating Effectively:** Recognize the importance of delegation in alleviating overwhelming responsibilities. Distribute tasks based on team members' strengths, allowing you to focus on strategic decision-making.
- **Building a Supportive Network:** Cultivate a supportive network of peers, mentors, or fellow introverted leaders. Share experiences, seek advice, and build a community that understands the nuances of introverted leadership.
- **Connect Upwards:** Engage with senior leaders to enhance your visibility and establish your presence as a leader.

Strategies for Work-Life Balance

- **Define Boundaries:** Establish clear boundaries between work and personal life. Communicate these boundaries to colleagues and superiors to ensure a balance that prioritizes both professional and personal commitments.
- **Prioritize Self-Care:** Recognize the importance of self-care and make it a priority. Engage in activities that recharge your energy, whether it's reading, drawing, or spending time in nature.
- **Create a Calming Workspace:** Design a workspace that aligns with your introverted preferences. Include elements that promote focus and reduce stress, such as soft lighting, comfortable seating, or soothing colors.
- **Schedule Breaks for Recharge:** Intentionally schedule breaks throughout the day to recharge. Whether it's a short walk, a moment of meditation, or peaceful reflection, these breaks can enhance productivity and well-being.

- **Negotiate Flexibility:** Advocate for flexible work arrangements that suit your introverted needs. Whether it's remote work options or adjusted work hours, negotiating flexibility can contribute to a healthier work-life balance.

Stories of Introverted Leaders from India and Beyond

In a world often enamored with extroverted charisma, the stories of introverted leaders stand out as a testament to the power of subdued fortitude and thoughtful leadership. From India to the global stage, these leaders have defied stereotypes and demonstrated that introversion can be a source of remarkable success and profound impact. Let's explore the journeys of both Indian and global leaders who, despite their introverted nature, have left an indelible mark on their respective fields and inspired countless others along the way.

Dr. A.P.J. Abdul Kalam:

- Known as the "Missile Man of India," he was a visionary scientist and the 11th President of India.
- Introverted Qualities: Dr. Kalam's humility, deep introspection, and quiet determination were hallmarks of his leadership style.
- Achievements: Dr. Kalam played a pivotal role in India's missile and space programs, contributing significantly to the country's technological advancements.
- Legacy: His legacy continues to inspire generations of Indians to dream big and pursue excellence with dedication and humility.

N. R. Narayana Murthy:

- Co-founder of Infosys, a pioneer in India's IT industry and a globally respected business leader.

- Introverted Qualities: Murthy's quiet demeanor, sharp intellect, and ethical values have been central to his leadership approach.
- Achievements: Under Murthy's leadership, Infosys grew into one of the world's largest IT services companies, revolutionizing the global outsourcing industry.
- Legacy: Murthy's journey from humble beginnings to corporate success serves as a beacon of inspiration for aspiring entrepreneurs and leaders.

Ratan Tata:

- Former Chairman of Tata Sons, a revered figure in India's business landscape and a leading philanthropist.
- Introverted Qualities: Despite his reserved nature, Tata is known for his compassionate leadership and strategic vision.
- Achievements: Under Tata's stewardship, the Tata Group expanded globally and became synonymous with integrity and social responsibility.
- Legacy: Tata's philanthropic initiatives, including the Tata Trusts, have transformed countless lives and inspired a culture of giving back.

Nirmala Sitharaman:

- Minister of Finance and Corporate Affairs of India, serving as a key figure in the country's economic policymaking.
- Introverted Qualities: Despite her high-profile role, Sitharaman maintains a reserved demeanor and is known for her meticulous approach to governance and policymaking.
- Achievements: Sitharaman has played a crucial role in steering India's economy through various challenges, including the COVID-19 pandemic and economic reforms.

- Legacy: As one of India's most prominent female leaders, Sitharaman's leadership exemplifies resilience, pragmatism, and a commitment to public service.

Indra Nooyi:

- An Indian-American business executive who served as the CEO and Chairperson of PepsiCo.
- Introverted Qualities: Nooyi's quiet determination, strategic acumen, and focus on long-term growth were key to her success.
- Achievements: Under Nooyi's leadership, PepsiCo diversified its product portfolio, expanded globally, and prioritized sustainability initiatives.
- Legacy: Nooyi's trailblazing career has inspired women and aspiring leaders around the world, breaking barriers, and challenging conventional norms.

Satya Nadella:

- CEO of Microsoft, one of the world's largest and most influential technology companies.
- Introverted Qualities: Known for his quiet demeanor and introspective nature, Nadella's leadership style is characterized by empathy, humility, and a focus on innovation.
- Achievements: Under Nadella's leadership, Microsoft has undergone a significant transformation, embracing cloud computing, artificial intelligence, and other emerging technologies.
- Legacy: Nadella's tenure as CEO has been marked by a renewed sense of purpose and vision, positioning Microsoft as a leader in the rapidly evolving tech landscape.

Bill Gates:

- Co-founder of Microsoft Corporation, one of the world's leading technology companies, and is also known for his philanthropic efforts through the Bill & Melinda Gates Foundation.

- Introverted Qualities: Gates is known for his introverted tendencies, often preferring quiet reflection and focused problem-solving over public attention.

- Achievements: Gates played a pivotal role in revolutionizing the personal computing industry with the development of Microsoft Windows and Office software. Additionally, through the Bill & Melinda Gates Foundation, he has made significant contributions to global health, education, and poverty alleviation.

- Legacy: Gates' legacy extends beyond the realm of technology, encompassing his philanthropic endeavors aimed at addressing some of the world's most pressing challenges. His commitment to using technology for social good and his advocacy for global health initiatives have earned him widespread recognition and admiration.

Angela Merkel:

- Served as the Chancellor of Germany for 16 years, making her one of the longest-serving leaders in modern European history.

- Introverted Qualities: Merkel is known for her calm demeanor, analytical approach, and ability to build consensus behind-the-scenes.

- Achievements: Merkel played a pivotal role in navigating Europe through numerous crises, including the Eurozone debt crisis and the refugee crisis.

- Legacy: Her leadership style, characterized by pragmatism and resilience, has earned her widespread respect and admiration both in Germany and abroad.

Warren Buffett:

- One of the most successful investors of all time and the chairman and CEO of Berkshire Hathaway.
- Introverted Qualities: Despite his immense wealth and influence, Buffett maintains a low-key lifestyle and prefers to let his investment decisions speak for themselves.
- Achievements: Buffett's value investing philosophy and long-term approach have made him a billionaire many times over and earned him the nickname "Oracle of Omaha."
- Legacy: Buffett's emphasis on integrity, patience, and rational decision-making has made him a role model for investors and business leaders worldwide.

Barack Obama:

- Served as the 44th President of the United States, becoming the first African American to hold the office.
- Introverted Qualities: Obama is known for his introspective nature, eloquent speech, and ability to connect with people on a personal level.
- Achievements: During his presidency, Obama implemented significant policy reforms, including the Affordable Care Act and the Paris Agreement on climate change.
- Legacy: Obama's leadership style, characterized by empathy and inclusivity, continues to inspire millions around the world, earning him accolades as a transformative leader.

Margaret Thatcher:

- Prime Minister of the United Kingdom from 1979 to 1990, making her the country's longest-serving Prime Minister of the 20th century.

- Introverted Qualities: Despite her strong public persona, Thatcher was known for her introverted tendencies, often preferring solitary decision-making and deep reflection.

- Achievements: Thatcher's tenure as Prime Minister saw significant economic reforms, privatization initiatives, and geopolitical shifts, earning her the nickname "Iron Lady."

- Legacy: Thatcher's leadership legacy continues to be debated, with supporters praising her resolve and vision, while critics point to the social and economic consequences of her policies.

Jacinda Ardern:

- Prime Minister of New Zealand, known for her empathetic leadership style and progressive policies.

- Introverted Qualities: Despite her public role, Ardern maintains a grounded and empathetic demeanor, often prioritizing listening, and consensus-building in her approach to governance.

- Achievements: Ardern's leadership during crises such as the Christchurch mosque shootings and the COVID-19 pandemic has earned her international acclaim for her compassion and effective crisis management.

- Legacy: Ardern's leadership legacy is characterized by a commitment to kindness, inclusivity, and social justice, making her a role model for leaders around the world.

Tim Cook:

- CEO of Apple Inc., one of the world's most valuable and iconic technology companies.
- Introverted Qualities: Cook is known for his quiet and reserved demeanor, preferring to lead by example and focus on long-term strategy rather than seeking the spotlight.
- Achievements: Under Cook's leadership, Apple has continued to innovate and grow, expanding its product line-up, services, and global reach.
- Legacy: Cook's commitment to privacy, sustainability, and social responsibility has solidified Apple's reputation as a leader in corporate ethics and innovation.

As we celebrate the achievements of these contemporary introverted leaders, both from India and around the world, we are reminded that leadership comes in many forms. Whether through quiet introspection, empathetic listening, or strategic vision, these leaders have demonstrated that introversion is not a barrier to success but a unique strength to be embraced and celebrated. As they continue to inspire change and make a positive impact on the world, their stories serve as a source of inspiration for aspiring leaders everywhere, proving that quiet strength and thoughtful leadership can truly change the world for the better.

"As a beacon of quiet strength, I lead with authenticity, guiding others with a steady hand and a compassionate heart."

Step 7: Sustaining Long-Term Success as an Introvert

"Rooted in resilience, my journey knows no bounds
as I cultivate a legacy of impact, endurance, and fulfillment."

Welcome to step 7 of your transformative journey, where we delve into the essential elements of sustaining long-term success as an introvert. In this step, we embark on a profound exploration of personal and professional development, equipping you with the tools and strategies to navigate the complex landscape of the modern workplace. From setting ambitious yet attainable goals to crafting a comprehensive career growth plan, we empower you to chart a course toward fulfillment and achievement. By cultivating a supportive network, understanding your introverted energy dynamics, and creating your ideal work environment, you'll discover the keys to unlocking your full potential and thriving in your chosen path. Additionally, we delve into effective stress management techniques, offer insights on navigating extrovert-dominated environments, and advocate for your introvert needs and preferences. Let's embark on this empowering journey toward sustained success, resilience, and fulfillment as an introvert in today's dynamic world.

An ancient tree with deep roots and lush foliage, signifying the long-term growth and success achievable through perseverance and continual self-development.

Why is it important for introverts to consider sustained success in the long run?

For introverts, long-term success in professional environments often hinges on understanding and leveraging their unique traits. The aspects listed below are essential as they align with introverted tendencies and enhance workplace effectiveness, ensuring that introverts not only survive but thrive in various settings:

- **Goal Setting and Career Planning**: This involves setting clear personal and professional objectives and developing a strategic career growth plan. It is crucial for introverts to have a roadmap that guides their progress and aligns with their inner values and strengths.

- **Building Networks and Advocating for Introvert Needs**: Introverts must cultivate supportive relationships that respect their working style and advocate for their needs in the workplace. This ensures they can secure opportunities and accommodations that allow them to perform optimally.

- **Managing Energy and Designing Ideal Workspaces**: Understanding and managing one's energy levels is vital for introverts, who may deplete their energy in crowded settings. Creating a work environment tailored to personal preferences can significantly boost productivity and job satisfaction.

- **Stress Management in Extrovert-Dominated Settings**: Learning to manage stress effectively, especially in environments that favor extroverted behavior, is key. This skill helps introverts navigate challenging social interactions and assert their space in the workplace.

These strategic aspects form a comprehensive framework that empowers introverts to harness their inherent qualities for sustained professional success and personal fulfillment. These aspects are covered here in detail.

Goal Setting and Career Planning

Setting Personal and Professional Goals

Let's talk about setting goals and how it can really amp up your game in the workplace. Sure, it might seem daunting at first, but trust me, with the right mindset and strategies, you'll be surprised at what you can achieve.

First things first, setting goals gives you a roadmap to follow. It helps you focus your energy on the things that really matter and gives you a clear sense of direction. Plus, it's a great way to channel your inner strengths and make a real impact in your workplace.

Now, when it comes to setting goals, it's all about being true to yourself. Take some time to reflect on what really lights you up. What are your values, strengths, and passions? Once you've figured that out, setting goals that align with who you are becomes a whole lot easier.

But here's the thing: you've got to keep it real. Sure, we introverts can be super detail-oriented, but that doesn't mean you have to aim for the stars right off the bat. Finding that balance between challenging yourself and setting achievable goals is key. Trust me, it'll save you from feeling overwhelmed and keep you on track to success.

Don't forget to mix it up with both short-term and long-term goals. Those short-term wins can really boost your confidence and keep you motivated. And those long-term goals? Well, they're like your North Star, guiding you toward your ultimate vision for your career.

One more thing – don't be afraid to share your goals with someone you trust. Whether it's a mentor, coach, or colleague, getting some outside perspective can be a game-changer. Plus, it helps keep you accountable and on track.

Set some goals and show the world what you're capable of. With the right goals in place, there's no limit to what you can achieve. Let's do this!

In conclusion, setting personal and professional goals is a vital strategy for you to accelerate your success in the workplace. By aligning your goals with your values, setting realistic targets, and seeking support from others, you can harness your unique strengths and talents to excel in your career. With proper goal setting, you can confidently navigate the workplace, make meaningful contributions, and achieve your desired outcomes.

Actions for You to Take:

Setting Personal and Professional Goals

- **Reflect on Your Values and Passions:** Spend 30 minutes journaling about your core values and long-term aspirations.

    - Your core values:

    ____

    ____

    - Your long-term aspirations:

    ____

    ____

- **Assess Your Strengths and Skills:** Create a list of your top five strengths and brainstorm how you can leverage them in your career.

- What are your top five strengths, and how can you leverage them in your career?

1.

2.

3.

4.

5.

- **Set SMART Goals:** Develop three SMART goals for the next six months, focusing on career advancement or skill development.
  - 3 SMART goals for the next six months, focusing on career advancement or skill development.

    1.

    2.

    3.

Developing Your Career Growth Plan

Let's talk about plotting out your career journey. As an introvert, having a solid plan in place can really give you that extra boost you need to thrive in the workplace.

What makes you shine? I'm talking about your strengths, skills, and interests. As introverts, we've got some pretty cool qualities, like our deep focus and killer listening skills. Take some time to figure out what sets you apart and how you can make the most of those strengths in your career.

Now, onto the fun part – setting some goals. And not just any goals; we're talking about SMART goals here. That means they're specific, measurable, attainable, relevant, and time-bound. Whether it's snagging that promotion or mastering a new skill, having clear goals gives you a roadmap to follow and keeps you focused.

Alright, let's talk networking. I know it's not exactly our favorite thing to do, but trust me, it's worth it. Look for networking opportunities that feel comfortable to you, whether it's joining a small group or diving into online communities. Building those connections can open up all sorts of doors and give you some awesome support along the way.

Now, here's where we really shine – introspection. We introverts thrive in those moments of reflection, so make sure to carve out some time for yourself. Use that time to check in on your progress, learn from your experiences, and tweak your plan as needed. And don't be afraid to reach out for feedback – sometimes an outside perspective can really help us see things in a new light.

So, there you have it – your personalized guide to career growth as an introvert. With a solid plan, a focus on your strengths, and a little bit of networking magic, there's no limit to what you can achieve. Let's do this!

Actions for you to take:

- **Identify Opportunities:** Attend at least one industry-related networking event or seminar in the next month.
- **Seek Mentorship:** Reach out to a potential mentor and schedule a coffee meeting to discuss your career aspirations.
- **Continuous Learning:** Enroll in an online course or workshop to develop a new skill or deepen your expertise in a specific area.

Building Networks and Advocating for Introvert Needs

Cultivating Your Supportive Network

Let's discuss building your support network – it's key for introverts like us to have people who get where we're coming from.

First up, finding fellow introverts. Look for those who understand your vibe and can offer some solid empathy. You can find them in professional networks, industry events, or even online communities tailored just for us introverts. These spaces are gold mines for swapping stories, seeking advice, and making some real connections.

Now, onto the extroverts. Yes, I said it – they may be a different breed, but they've got a lot to offer. Take the time to really listen to them, show interest in what they're all about, and engage in some meaningful conversations. Building bridges like this creates a network that's rich, diverse, and totally supportive of your growth.

Next on the list are mentors and sponsors. These folks are like career fairy godparents. Seek out those who've been there and done that in your field and share some of your introverted tendencies. Mentors can give you killer advice and help you navigate the workplace maze, while sponsors can really push your career forward by advocating for you and opening up new opportunities.

Last but not least, let's talk about honing those communication and networking skills. Sure, introverts are great listeners, but sometimes we need to amp up our speaking game, too. Get out there, attend some networking events, and practice your small talk. Finding your groove in these situations helps you share your ideas, make connections, and build that killer support network.

In conclusion, cultivating a supportive network is crucial for you as an introverted employee looking to excel in the workplace. By finding like-minded individuals, building relationships with extroverts, seeking mentors and sponsors, and developing communication skills, you can create a community that not only understands your unique needs but also propels your professional success. With the right support system, you can thrive in your career and make a lasting impact in your chosen field.

Actions for You to Take:

- **Find Like-minded Individuals:** Join an online forum or LinkedIn group for introverted professionals and introduce yourself to the community.
- **Build Relationships with Extroverts:** Invite an extroverted colleague to lunch or a coffee meeting to discuss a project or idea.
- **Connect with Mentors and Sponsors:** Identify three potential mentors or sponsors within your organization or industry and reach out to schedule informational interviews.

Advocating for Your Introvert Needs and Preferences

It can often feel like introverts are left to fend for themselves in the workplace. However, as an introvert, it is crucial for you to recognize and advocate for your unique needs and preferences in order to thrive and excel in your career. Let me shed light on the importance of advocating for introvert needs and provide strategies to accelerate your success at the workplace.

- **Recognize Your Value:** Firstly, it is crucial to understand that being an introvert is not a disadvantage but rather a valuable trait. You possess numerous strengths that can contribute to your success, such as thoughtful decision-making, deep focus, and excellent listening skills. However, in order to harness these strengths, it is essential to create an environment that supports your introvert needs.

- **Effective Communication**: One way to advocate for your introvert needs is through effective communication. You often prefer written communication over verbal exchanges, as it allows you to carefully craft your thoughts and express yourself more comfortably. Make this preference known to colleagues and managers to ensure that you are given opportunities to communicate through written channels, such as emails or project updates.

- **Setting Boundaries**: Another important aspect of advocating for your introvert needs is setting boundaries. You thrive in quiet and solitude, which allows you to recharge and process information. Communicate the need for uninterrupted work time and establish boundaries that protect this vital aspect of your well-being. This can be achieved by scheduling quiet hours, creating designated quiet spaces, or politely declining unnecessary social engagements that drain your energy.

- **Prioritize Meaningful Connections**: Furthermore, you often prefer deeper connections and meaningful conversations over small talk. Advocate for this preference by seeking out opportunities for one-on-one conversations or participating in smaller group discussions where more substantial ideas can be exchanged. By focusing on quality over quantity, you can forge stronger professional relationships and make a more significant impact.

Ultimately, advocating for your introverted needs and preferences is about embracing and celebrating your unique strengths. By understanding your needs and effectively communicating them to others, you can create a workplace environment that fosters your success. Remember, being an introvert is not a hindrance but a valuable asset that can drive exceptional performance and accelerate your success at the workplace.

Managing Energy and Designing Ideal Workspaces

Managing Energy: Understanding Your Introvert Energy Dynamics

Let's understand your energy dynamics as an introvert. It's all about recognizing your strengths and knowing how to navigate in a world that often seems tailor-made for extroverts.

First thing – honor your need for alone time. While extroverts thrive on social interactions, you recharge by having some quality solo moments. Making space for quiet reflection is like giving your batteries a much-needed boost, so don't skimp on it.

Now, let's talk about managing sensory overload. You're sensitive to your surroundings, which means noisy or chaotic environments can easily throw you off balance. Setting up your workspace with a cozy nook or some noise-canceling headphones can work wonders. And don't forget to set boundaries – letting your colleagues know when you need uninterrupted focus time can help keep distractions at bay.

Understanding your energy levels throughout the day is key. After a long meeting or a deep dive into a project, you might feel your energy taking a nosedive, isn't it? Recognizing these patterns allows you to plan your day accordingly so you can tackle tasks when you're at your best.

When it comes to teamwork, lean into your strengths. Your thoughtful listening skills and knack for deep thinking make you a valuable asset to any group. Jump into discussions, use your analytical chops to dissect problems, and don't be shy about sharing your ideas – your unique perspective can make a big difference.

Last but not least, don't hesitate to speak up for yourself. Educating your colleagues and managers about introverted energy dynamics can lead to a more supportive work environment. Whether it's advocating for quiet spaces or pushing for flexible work arrangements, making your needs known is essential for thriving as an introvert in the workplace.

In conclusion, understanding your introvert energy dynamics is a crucial step toward excelling in the workplace. By embracing your need for solitude, managing sensory input, optimizing your schedule, leveraging your strengths, and advocating for yourself, you can tap into your full potential and accelerate your success at work. Remember, being an introvert is not a weakness but a powerful advantage when harnessed effectively.

Actions for you to take:

- **Schedule Downtime:** Reserve 15 minutes of quiet time on your calendar each morning and afternoon for reflection and relaxation.
- **Set Boundaries:** Have a conversation with your manager about establishing guidelines for interruptions and respecting focused work time.
- **Practice Mindfulness:** Dedicate five minutes each day to mindfulness practice, focusing on your breath and observing your thoughts without judgment.

Creating Your Ideal Work Environment

Meet Harish, a diligent introvert navigating his way through the corporate world. Despite his reserved nature, Harish knew that his unique qualities held the key to his success. He embarked on a journey to create his ideal work environment tailored to his introverted needs.

- *First, Harish prioritized understanding his own requirements. Recognizing his need for solitude, he made it a point to carve out moments of quiet reflection during his workday. Whether it was finding a cozy corner in the office or taking short breaks for contemplation, Harish understood the importance of recharging his energy levels.*

- *Next, Harish tackled the challenge of minimizing distractions. Aware that open office layouts and constant interruptions hindered his focus, he took proactive steps to mitigate these distractions. Armed with noise-canceling headphones and a request for a quieter workspace, Harish created an environment conducive to deep concentration. He also set clear boundaries with his colleagues, communicating his need for uninterrupted focus time.*

- *Despite his preference for solo work, Harish recognized the value of collaboration. When working in groups, he adeptly communicated his preferences for structured teamwork. By suggesting alternative methods, such as written communication or individual reflection before group discussions, Harish ensured his ideas were effectively conveyed while respecting his introverted nature.*

- *Harish's strength lay in his ability for deep thinking and reflection. He integrated opportunities for introspection into his daily routine, setting aside time for journaling, planning, and goal setting.*

> *Through these practices, Harish tapped into his introverted strengths, fostering both personal and professional growth.*
> - *Lastly, Harish understood that the ideal work environment extended beyond physical factors to encompass company culture. He sought out organizations that valued introverted qualities such as thoughtful decision-making and active listening. By surrounding himself with like-minded individuals and supportive colleagues, Harish found himself thriving in an environment that celebrated his introverted nature, enhancing his job satisfaction and overall success.*

As an introvert, it's crucial to create an ideal work environment that allows you to thrive. By understanding your own needs, minimizing distractions, advocating for collaboration approaches that suit you, incorporating introspection, and seeking out supportive company cultures, you can accelerate your success at the workplace. Embrace your introverted strengths and confidently excel in your career.

Actions for You to Take:

- **Optimize Your Physical Space:** De-clutter your desk and add personal touches or calming elements such as plants or ambient lighting.
- **Advocate for Flexible Work Arrangements:** Research your company's policies on flexible work arrangements and schedule a meeting with HR to explore available options.
- **Promote Inclusive Collaboration:** Volunteer to facilitate a team meeting or brainstorming session using structured techniques that ensure equal participation from all team members.

Stress Management in Extrovert-Dominated Settings
Implementing Effective Stress Management Techniques

As an introvert, you often face unique challenges in the workplace, where the demands of social interaction and constant stimulation can be draining. However, by implementing effective stress management techniques, you can not only navigate these challenges but also excel in your career. Let's explore some strategies specifically tailored to introverts to help you accelerate your success at the workplace.

- Embrace solitude: You thrive in quiet and reflective environments. Find ways to create moments of solitude throughout your workday, whether it's taking short breaks in a quiet corner or finding a peaceful spot during lunchtime. Solitude allows you to recharge and regain focus, ultimately enhancing productivity and reducing stress.
- Prioritize self-care: Taking care of yourself is essential for maintaining your energy levels and mental well-being. Make self-care a priority by engaging in activities that bring you joy and relaxation outside of work. This could include reading a book, practicing yoga, or pursuing a hobby. By dedicating time to recharge, you can better manage stress and maintain a healthy work-life balance.
- Set boundaries: It's easy for you to become overwhelmed by continuous demands for your time and attention. Learn to set clear boundaries and communicate them effectively to colleagues and supervisors. This could involve scheduling uninterrupted work periods, setting limits on social engagements, or politely declining excessive workloads. Setting boundaries allows you to manage your energy more effectively and avoid burnout.

- Practice mindfulness: Mindfulness is a powerful tool for managing stress and remaining present in the workplace. By cultivating awareness of your thoughts and emotions, you can better regulate your responses to stressful situations. Incorporate mindfulness practices, such as deep breathing exercises or short meditation sessions, into your daily routines to foster calmness and resilience.

- Seek support: Building a network of like-minded individuals can provide you with a sense of belonging and support. Connect with other introverts in the workplace, either through informal gatherings or professional associations. Sharing experiences and strategies with individuals who understand the challenges introverts face can be immensely helpful in reducing stress and boosting confidence.

By implementing these effective stress management techniques, you can navigate the workplace with greater ease and accelerate your success. Remember, introversion is a strength, and by embracing it and taking care of yourself, you can excel in your chosen career while maintaining your mental well-being.

Actions for You to Take:

- **Embrace Self-Care:** Create a weekly self-care routine that includes activities such as exercise, hobbies, and relaxation techniques.

- **Establish Healthy Boundaries:** Practice saying "no" to non-essential requests or commitments that may overwhelm or deplete your resources.

- **Seek Support:** Schedule regular check-ins with a friend or family member to discuss your stressors and explore coping strategies together.

Navigating Extrovert-Dominated and Fast-Paced Environments

Extroverts excel in networking, public speaking, and assertiveness, seemingly effortlessly navigating through extrovert-driven and fast-paced cultures. But what about you as an introvert? How can you not only survive but also thrive in these environments? Let's explore strategies and insights tailored specifically for introverts who want to accelerate their success at the workplace.

- **Find Your Voice**: While extroverts may naturally assert themselves in group settings, you can make your mark by focusing on quality over quantity. Cultivate your listening skills and contribute thoughtful, well-crafted ideas during meetings or discussions. Your insights and unique perspectives will stand out and make a lasting impact.

- **Effective Communication and Establishing Clear Expectations:** Embrace written communication when possible, allowing for thoughtful responses. Prepare and rehearse key points for verbal communication to enhance confidence. Communicate preferences and needs to colleagues and superiors. Establish realistic expectations regarding response times and project deadlines.

- **Preparation and Reflection**: Use your strengths in preparation and reflection to your advantage. Before important meetings or presentations, take the time to thoroughly prepare and rehearse. Afterwards, reflect on your performance and identify areas for improvement. This dedication to self-improvement will set you apart and demonstrate your commitment to excellence.

- **Networking**: Networking, a key aspect of success in any workplace, may seem daunting for introverts. However, you have a natural inclination toward forming deep connections with others. Leverage this by cultivating a smaller, meaningful network of colleagues and mentors who appreciate your thoughtful approach. You can start with one-on-one meetings or attend smaller events. Quality relationships will yield valuable opportunities and support.

- **Finding Balance**: In environments dominated by extroverted energy, introverts may find themselves feeling drained. Prioritizing self-care becomes paramount. Regular breaks and engaging in activities that rejuvenate are essential. Establishing boundaries to preserve energy is crucial for sustained productivity and well-being. Integrate structured breaks into your workday, utilizing this time for solitary activities that offer a mental reset, allowing you to return to work refreshed and focused.

- **Prioritization and Time Management:** Develop a systematic approach to prioritize tasks and manage time effectively. Break down larger projects into smaller, manageable tasks to maintain focus.

- **Mindfulness and Stress Management:** Incorporate mindfulness techniques to stay present and manage stress. Identify stress triggers and implement coping mechanisms, such as short breaks or deep breathing exercises.

As an introvert, you can successfully navigate extrovert-dominated and fast-paced environments by leveraging your strengths and implementing strategic approaches. By focusing on effective communication, meaningful networking, and prioritizing self-care, you can excel in your career while maintaining balance and well-being. Embracing these strategies enables you to thrive professionally and contribute positively to your organization.

Overcoming Stereotypes and Challenges

Embrace Sociability as an Introvert

- **Connect:** Break free from the stereotype of introverts avoiding socializing. Dedicate a few minutes daily to office networking to build connections and make your presence known.
- **Adapt & Thrive:** Learn flexibility and adaptability. Show different facets of your personality based on the context without compromising your core values.

Smile, Walk, Talk

- **Smile:** Leverage the power of a smile to appear approachable and positive in a corporate environment.
- **Walk:** Embrace confident body language with straight posture, eye contact, and a head held high to communicate self-assurance.
- **Talk:** Master the art of expressing yourself by avoiding fast speech, articulating words, and paying attention to your tone of voice.

Summary of Actions for you to take:

Setting Personal and Professional Goals

- **Reflect on Your Values and Passions:** Spend 30 minutes journaling about your core values and long-term aspirations.
- **Assess Your Strengths and Skills:** Create a list of your top five strengths and brainstorm how you can leverage them in your career.

- **Set SMART Goals:** Develop three SMART goals for the next six months, focusing on career advancement or skill development.

Developing a Career Growth Plan

- **Identify Opportunities:** Attend at least one industry-related networking event or seminar in the next month.
- **Seek Mentorship:** Reach out to a potential mentor and schedule a coffee meeting to discuss your career aspirations.
- **Continuous Learning:** Enroll in an online course or workshop to develop a new skill or deepen your expertise in a specific area.

Cultivating a Supportive Network

- **Find Like-minded Individuals:** Join an online forum or LinkedIn group for introverted professionals and introduce yourself to the community.
- **Build Relationships with Extroverts:** Invite an extroverted colleague to lunch or a coffee meeting to discuss a project or idea.
- **Connect with Mentors and Sponsors:** Identify three potential mentors or sponsors within your organization or industry and reach out to schedule informational interviews.

Managing Your Energy and Avoiding Burnout

- **Schedule Downtime:** Reserve 15 minutes of quiet time on your calendar each morning and afternoon for reflection and relaxation.
- **Set Boundaries:** Have a conversation with your manager about establishing guidelines for interruptions and respecting focused work time.

- **Practice Mindfulness:** Dedicate five minutes each day to mindfulness practice, focusing on your breath and observing your thoughts without judgment.

Creating Your Ideal Work Environment

- **Optimize Your Physical Space:** De-clutter your desk and add personal touches or calming elements such as plants or ambient lighting.
- **Advocate for Flexible Work Arrangements:** Research your company's policies on flexible work arrangements and schedule a meeting with HR to explore available options.
- **Promote Inclusive Collaboration:** Volunteer to facilitate a team meeting or brainstorming session using structured techniques that ensure equal participation from all team members.

Implementing Effective Stress Management Techniques

- **Embrace Self-Care:** Create a weekly self-care routine that includes activities such as exercise, hobbies, and relaxation techniques.
- **Establish Healthy Boundaries:** Practice saying "no" to non-essential requests or commitments that may overwhelm or deplete your resources.
- **Seek Support:** Schedule regular check-ins with a friend or family member to discuss your stressors and explore coping strategies together.

Chapter 5

Opportunities for Introverts to be Successful

Introverts can sometimes feel overlooked or misunderstood in their quest for success; however, the opportunities for introverts to thrive are more abundant than ever before. From navigating career advancement in traditional corporate settings to exploring introvert-friendly job options and even charting a course as an entrepreneur, there's a wealth of pathways for introverts to achieve their goals and reach new heights of success.

Let's delve into the strategies and opportunities available for introverts to carve out their own unique paths to success, whether within established organizations or as entrepreneurs forging their own destinies. Let's explore how introverts can leverage their unique strengths, navigate challenges, and chart a course toward fulfilling and successful careers.

In this chapter, we will cover the following topics: Navigating Career Advancement, Exploring Introvert-Friendly Jobs, and Navigating Success as an Introverted Entrepreneur.

Navigating Career Advancement

Advancing in your career requires mastering essential skills and adopting strategic approaches. As an introvert, you possess unique qualities that can be leveraged to excel in the workplace. Let's explore key strategies tailored to introverted individuals seeking to advance their careers.

- **Deliver Results:**

  - Leverage introverted qualities such as active listening to build positive relationships with colleagues and supervisors. Demonstrating your reliability and competence fosters trust and respect, paving the way for career growth.
  - Adapt to your manager's preferences and focus on consistently delivering high-quality results. Your attention to detail and ability to work independently can be invaluable assets in achieving success.

- **Show Potential:**

  - Concentrate on actions that accelerate your professional growth, such as expanding your skill set and actively seeking feedback on your performance. Use introspection to identify your strengths and areas for improvement, guiding your development efforts effectively.
  - Take initiative in pursuing learning opportunities and professional development activities. By continuously enhancing your skills and knowledge, you position yourself as a proactive and valuable contributor within your organization.

- **Gain Advocacy:**

  - Support and uplift your colleagues generously, leveraging your strong observation skills to identify opportunities for assistance. Actively contribute to team efforts and offer your expertise to help others succeed.
  - Cultivate positive relationships with co-workers and supervisors by demonstrating your reliability, integrity,

and willingness to collaborate. By fostering goodwill and camaraderie, you gain advocates who can support and champion your career advancement.

- **Foster Strong Friendships:**

  - Capitalize on your strengths in one-on-one interactions to establish meaningful relationships with colleagues and mentors. Take the time to connect authentically with others, demonstrating empathy and understanding.

  - Build a coalition of supporters within your organization who can advocate for your advancement and provide guidance and encouragement along the way. By nurturing strong friendships and alliances, you enhance your visibility and support network within the workplace.

- **Seek Mentorship:**

  - Actively seek out mentorship opportunities within your organization or industry. Identify individuals whose career trajectories you admire and approach them for guidance and advice.

  - Engage in regular discussions with your mentors to gain insights into navigating your career path effectively and overcoming potential challenges.

- **Continuously Learn and Develop:**

  - Embrace a mindset of lifelong learning and professional development. Stay abreast of industry trends, technological advancements, and best practices relevant to your field.

  - Invest time and effort in acquiring new skills and competencies that are in demand within your industry, positioning yourself as a valuable asset to your organization.

By incorporating these essential strategies into your approach to career advancement, you can leverage your introverted qualities to thrive in the workplace and achieve your professional goals. Remember, success is not solely determined by extroverted traits but by the strategic utilization of your unique strengths and capabilities.

Exploring Introvert-Friendly Jobs

Choosing a career path that aligns with your introverted strengths is essential for long-term success and satisfaction in the workplace. As introverts, you possess a unique set of qualities that can be leveraged to thrive in various professional environments.

The guidance below is rooted in characteristics commonly associated with introverted individuals: good listeners, focused, observant, compassionate leaders, independent, disciplined, empathetic, analytically minded, creative, attentive to detail, strong relationships, adaptable, and self-reliant.

Choosing the Right Job:

When exploring employment opportunities as an introvert, it's crucial to prioritize roles that not only align with your strengths but also energize rather than drain you. Consider the following strategies:

- Limiting Social Interactions: You can opt for roles that involve limited social interactions, such as graphic design or writing, allowing you to focus on tasks that play to your strengths.
- Remote Work: Explore opportunities for remote work, which can minimize draining interactions and provide greater flexibility and autonomy in your work environment.
- Project-Based Assignments: Pursue projects and assignments that offer opportunities for independent and flexible work,

enabling you to work at your own pace and in environments conducive to your productivity.

While these strategies closely align with your personality, please note that you may need to step out of your comfort zone to pursue employment in areas that require a broader working style.

Introvert-Friendly Jobs:

It's essential to dispel the misconception that as an introverted individual, your career options are limited. In truth, there are plenty of exciting and fulfilling roles that align with your preferences and strengths. The key is recognizing your needs and finding a work environment that values your inclination toward independent work. Embracing your introverted qualities can open doors to success in various professions.

Introverts tend to thrive in job categories that allow for independent work, deep focus, and minimal social interaction. Here are a few categories of jobs where introverts often excel include:

- **Analytical/Financial Roles:** Jobs such as accountant, actuary, or data scientist involve tasks that require deep analysis, attention to detail, and independent problem-solving, which align well with introverted strengths.
  - **Accountant:** Introverts are well-suited to accounting roles due to their attention to detail and preference for meticulous tasks. They excel in tasks involving financial analysis, budgeting, and compliance.
  - **Actuary:** Actuaries assess risk and advise companies on financial decisions. Introverts' analytical prowess allows them to excel in analyzing complex data sets and minimizing financial risks for clients.
- **Information Technology (IT) Roles:** Careers like IT engineers, web developers, or technical helpdesk professionals

often involve working with technology and systems, which can be more solitary tasks, allowing introverts to work independently and solve technical problems.

- **IT Engineer:** Introverts thrive in roles that involve careful analysis and problem-solving, making IT engineering a natural fit. They contribute to the development, implementation, and management of secure IT solutions.

- **Web Developer:** Web development offers introverts the opportunity to work independently to build and maintain websites and applications. Their technical expertise and problem-solving skills are well-suited to creating user-friendly digital experiences.

- **Research and Writing:** Roles that involve research, writing, and content creation, such as researcher, writer, or editor, provide opportunities for introverts to work alone, delve deeply into topics of interest, and express their thoughts and ideas through written communication.

  - **Researcher:** Introverts excel in conducting thorough research and analysis to uncover meaningful insights. They contribute to driving advancements in their fields through their deep focus and dedication to uncovering new knowledge.

  - **Writer/Editor:** Writing and editing roles allow introverts to work alone to craft engaging content. Their creativity and language proficiency enable them to communicate ideas effectively through written communication.

- **Creative Fields:** While creativity-related roles like artist, graphic designer, or photographer may involve some collaboration and interaction, introverts can thrive in these areas because they often allow for focused, solitary work during the creative process.

- **Artist:** Introverts express their creativity through various mediums, showcasing their unique perspective and artistic talents. They often prefer solitary work environments where they can focus on their craft without distractions.
- **Graphic Designer/Photographer:** These roles involve creating visually appealing designs or capturing compelling images. Introverts leverage their creativity and a keen eye for detail to communicate messages effectively through visual media.
- **Healthcare and Social Services:** Certain roles in healthcare and social services, such as psychologist or social worker, involve meaningful one-on-one interactions with clients or patients, which introverts may find fulfilling because they can deeply connect with individuals on a personal level.
  - **Psychologist/Social Worker:** While these roles involve one-on-one interactions with clients or patients, introverts may find fulfillment in providing support and resources to address social and emotional challenges. They connect deeply with individuals and make meaningful contributions to their well-being.

In summary, introverts thrive in job roles that offer autonomy, deep focus, and opportunities for meaningful contributions. Whether it's through analytical tasks, creative endeavors, or helping others in healthcare and social services, introverts excel when they can work independently and leverage their unique strengths to make a positive impact in their chosen fields. As I have already mentioned, while it's true that certain industries and professions may seem tailor-made for introverted individuals, there's no need to confine oneself to these conventional paths. It's essential to dare to pursue a career aligned with one's passion, even if it means navigating a gap between one's inherent personality style and the requirements of a desired field. Success lies in the ability to adapt behaviors and strategies that enhance performance while remaining true to oneself.

Navigating Success as an Introverted Entrepreneur

Introverted entrepreneurs have proven that success knows no bounds when it comes to personality traits.

Let's explore the stories of renowned introverted entrepreneurs who have not only achieved significant success but also serve as inspiration for aspiring business leaders.

- Azim Premji: He is an Indian business tycoon, investor, and philanthropist who is the chairman of Wipro Limited. Despite his introverted nature, Premji has steered Wipro to become one of the largest IT services companies in India, with a global presence spanning multiple continents. His emphasis on ethical business practices and corporate social responsibility sets him apart as a visionary leader.

- Shiv Nadar: He is an Indian billionaire industrialist and philanthropist who is the founder and chairman of HCL Technologies, a multinational IT services company based in India. Despite being introverted, Nadar's strategic vision and leadership have propelled HCL to become one of the largest IT companies in India, with a strong focus on innovation and customer-centric solutions.

- Kiran Mazumdar-Shaw: She is an Indian billionaire entrepreneur and the founder of Biocon Limited, a biotechnology company based in Bangalore. Despite facing numerous challenges as a woman in a male-dominated industry, Mazumdar-Shaw's introverted nature did not deter her from pursuing her entrepreneurial ambitions. She has played a pioneering role in revolutionizing the biotechnology sector in India and has been recognized globally for her contributions to science and entrepreneurship.

- Larry Page: He is the co-founder of Google, stands as a testament to the fact that introversion is not a hindrance to success. Despite his reserved nature, Page's net worth of £93 billion as of February 2023 places him among the world's wealthiest individuals. Page's innovation extends beyond Google, as he invests in ground-breaking ventures like flying car firms Kitty Hawk and Opener.

- Mark Zuckerberg: As the co-founder of Facebook, Mark Zuckerberg has navigated challenges with a focus on customer service and innovation. His success in leading one of the world's most prominent tech companies demonstrates that introverted qualities, when harnessed effectively, can drive ground-breaking achievements.

- Elon Musk: Engineer and founder of SpaceX and Tesla Motors, Elon Musk, embraces introversion while pushing boundaries in aerospace and electric vehicles. Musk's commitment to innovation and sustainability reflects how introverted individuals can excel by staying true to their principles.

Please note that determining whether someone is an introvert can sometimes be speculative, as it's based on observable behaviors and characteristics rather than a formal diagnosis. However, in the cases mentioned above, there are several indicators that suggest these entrepreneurs may exhibit introverted traits:

- **Reserved Demeanor:** Many of these entrepreneurs are known for their reserved demeanor in public appearances and interactions, which is often associated with introversion.

- **Preference for Solitude:** Introverts typically prefer solitary activities or small group settings over large social gatherings or events. While not definitive, reports and anecdotes about these entrepreneurs often mention their preference for spending time alone or in smaller, more intimate settings.

- **Focus on Depth over Breadth:** Introverts tend to prioritize deep, meaningful relationships and pursuits over superficial interactions or activities. The dedication and focus exhibited by these entrepreneurs in their respective fields may suggest a preference for depth over breadth.

- **Reflective Nature:** Introverts often engage in introspection and reflection, spending time contemplating ideas and decisions before taking action. The strategic thinking and thoughtful approach demonstrated by these entrepreneurs align with introverted tendencies.

- **Limited Public Speaking:** While not always the case, introverts may feel less comfortable with public speaking or large-scale presentations compared to extroverts. While many of these entrepreneurs have undoubtedly delivered speeches and presentations, their demeanor during such events may offer insights into their comfort level with public engagement.

While we cannot definitively label these individuals as introverts without their self-identification or formal assessments, their behaviors and characteristics align with commonly observed traits of introversion.

Introverted entrepreneurs harness distinct strengths that propel success in the business arena. By embracing their inherent qualities, capitalizing on strengths, and employing strategic approaches, introverts can leave a significant imprint. The stories mentioned above aim to embolden introverts on their entrepreneurial path, highlighting that achievement is reachable without forsaking fundamental values.

The trajectory of introverted entrepreneurs underscores the richness of leadership diversity. Through recognizing and honoring introverted attributes, individuals enrich the business landscape with meaningful contributions.

Starting and Running Your Own Business

Entrepreneurship offers introverts the opportunity to create a work environment that aligns with their preferences. Many introverted individuals have successfully started and run their businesses, demonstrating that introversion can be a strength in the entrepreneurial world.

- **Passion-Driven Ventures:**

  - Pursue business ideas aligned with personal interests and passions.
  - Build a venture around a niche where introvert strengths can shine.

- **Solo Entrepreneurship:**

  - Consider solo entrepreneurship to maintain autonomy and control.
  - Leverage online platforms for marketing and customer interactions.

- **Strategic Networking:**

  - Focus on building a small but influential network of connections.
  - Prioritize quality relationships over quantity for business growth.

Leveraging Your Introvert Strengths

Introverted business owners can turn their inherent traits into powerful assets. Real-world examples illustrate how introverts have harnessed their strengths for success:

- **Innovative Thinking:**

  - Showcase how introverted introspection leads to innovative solutions.
  - Highlight instances where unique perspectives have driven business growth.

- **Deep Customer Understanding:**

  - Demonstrate the ability to deeply understand customer needs and preferences.
  - Use this understanding to tailor products or services for maximum impact.

- **Effective Leadership:**

  - Illustrate how introverted leaders excel in creating focused and efficient teams.
  - Showcase leadership styles that prioritize team well-being and collaboration.

- **Adaptable Decision-Making:**

  - Share examples of adaptable decision-making based on thoughtful analysis.
  - Highlight instances where introverted leaders have successfully navigated challenges.

Whispers of Innovation: Kalpana Raj's Subtle Revolution in Design Entrepreneurship

In the bustling metropolis of Pune, nestled in a quaint corner office flooded with the soft light of dawn, Kalpana Raj embarked on a journey that would defy the conventional bravado of entrepreneurship. An introvert by nature, Kalpana found her passion in the realm of graphic design, a field where her creativity could whisper louder than words. Despite the cacophony of doubts echoing the challenges of her reserved demeanor, Kalpana was determined to weave her introspection into the fabric of her own business.

__The Genesis of Vision:__ Kalpana's venture, "InNovate Design Studio," was born not out of a quest for fame but a genuine desire to craft visual stories that resonated. Her business idea, deeply rooted in her personal interest and passion for design, aimed to offer bespoke branding solutions for emerging start-ups. The niche was perfect—a realm where Kalpana's introverted strengths could not only shine but also thrive.

__Solo Entrepreneurship with a Twist:__ Recognizing the autonomy and control solo entrepreneurship afforded, Kalpana initially embarked on her journey alone. Yet, she was quick to understand that the essence of her strength lay not in solitude but in the strategic delegation of tasks that fell outside her zone of genius. Leveraging online platforms, she marketed her services, connecting with clients who valued depth over flamboyance.

__Strategic Networking and Team Building:__ Kalpana's networking strategy was unconventional yet impactful. She focused on forging a handful of meaningful connections rather than casting a wide net. Each relationship was nurtured with care, leading to collaborations that were as fruitful as they were fulfilling. Recognizing her need for complementary forces, Kalpana carefully assembled a team that mirrored the diversity of skills required to run a successful design studio. She sought individuals whose strengths offset her weaknesses—dynamic marketers, eloquent client *managers, and visionary designers who shared her ethos but brought their extroverted energy to the table.*

However, the journey was not without its hurdles. One significant challenge arose when InNovate Design Studio faced a critical client pitch, one that could elevate the studio to new heights. The client, accustomed to high-energy presentations and charismatic pitches, initially seemed underwhelmed by Kalpana's subdued but thoughtful approach. Doubts crept in, whispering that perhaps her introverted nature was a misfit in the flamboyant world of design entrepreneurship.

Leveraging Introvert Strengths: *Yet InNovate Design Studio quickly became known for its innovative solutions. Kalpana's introspection and deep customer understanding allowed her to tailor services that precisely met her clients' needs, often anticipating trends before they became mainstream. Her leadership style, though quiet, was fiercely effective. She fostered a work environment that prioritized well-being and collaboration, where each team member felt seen and valued.*

Determined to turn the tide, Kalpana focused on what she did best: diving deep into the client's needs and crafting a proposal that spoke volumes through its clarity and creativity. Her detailed presentation, rich with insights and customized solutions, eventually won the client over, proving that genuine innovation and understanding could indeed speak louder than the loudest pitch.

Adaptable Decision-Making: *Kalpana's path to success was punctuated by obstacles, each presenting its own set of challenges. However, her introverted nature equipped her with an adaptable decision-making process grounded in thoughtful analysis. Each challenge was met with calm deliberation, transforming potential setbacks into stepping stones for growth.*

InNovate Design Studio's success story was a testament to Kalpana's belief that introversion, often misconstrued as a barrier to entrepreneurship, was her undisputed strength. Her journey illuminated the path for countless other introverted entrepreneurs, showcasing that with the right blend of passion, strategic networking, and leveraging inherent strengths, the entrepreneurial dream was not only attainable but also ripe with the potential for unprecedented success.

Kalpana Raj, through her quiet resolve and innovative spirit, redefined entrepreneurship on her own terms, proving that even in the world of business, where extroversion is often celebrated, there is immense power in the quietude of introversion.

Business Ideas Tailored for Introverts

Here are a few business ideas that capitalize on the strengths of introverts, allowing them to work independently, utilize their creativity and analytical skills, and engage with others on their own terms. These are categorized based on their nature and industry focus:

- **Service-Based Businesses:**

    - Virtual Assistant Services
    - Consulting (e.g., Business, Marketing, Financial)
    - Coaching (e.g., Executive, Life, Health)
    - Social Media Management
    - Content Writing and Copywriting Services
    - Graphic Design Services
    - Bookkeeping Services
    - Translation Services
    - Health and Wellness Coaching
    - Personal Finance Planning

- **Skill-Based Businesses:**

    - Online Course Creation
    - Podcasting

- Software as a Service (SaaS) Development
- Photography Services
- Web Development and Design
- IT Support Services
- Content Curation Services

- **Creative Ventures:**

  - Niche Blogging
  - Freelance Writing
  - Artist or Artisan Ventures (e.g., Painting, Crafting)
  - Podcasting
  - Graphic Design Services

- **Retail and E-Commerce:**

  - Online Retail Arbitrage
  - E-Commerce Store Ownership

- **Specialized Industries:**

  - Healthcare Services (e.g., Telehealth, Wellness Coaching)
  - Financial Services (e.g., Bookkeeping, Personal Finance Planning)
  - Technology and Software Development (e.g., SaaS, Web Development)
  - Education and Training (e.g., Online Courses, Tutoring)
  - Creative Arts and Media (e.g., Blogging, Podcasting)
  - Language Services (e.g., Translation)
  - Personal Development and Coaching (e.g., Life Coaching, Health Coaching)

- **Digital Ventures:**

  - Online Course Creation
  - Podcasting

- • Software as a Service (SaaS) Development
- • Graphic Design Services
- • Web Development and Design
- • Content Writing and Copywriting Services
- • Blogging
- • Freelance Writing

- **Consulting and Coaching:**

  - • Consulting (Business, Marketing, Financial)
  - • Coaching (Executive, Life, Health)
  - • Social Media Management
  - • Health and Wellness Coaching
  - • Personal Finance Planning
  - • Executive Coaching

These ideas cover a wide range of industries and sectors, allowing introverts to find opportunities that align with their interests, skills, and preferences. With dedication and strategic planning, introverted entrepreneurs can successfully launch and grow their own businesses.

Vital Tips for Unleashing Your Introverted Entrepreneurial Spirit

In the bustling world of business, your introverted nature is not a hindrance but a unique advantage waiting to be unleashed. While the narrative often leans toward extroverted traits, your inherent strengths hold immense potential for entrepreneurial success. Here are invaluable tips tailored specifically for introverts like you to thrive in the dynamic business landscape:

- **Prioritize Your Well-being:** As an introverted entrepreneur, self-care is paramount. Nurture your mental and physical health, ensuring you have the energy and resilience needed for the entrepreneurial journey ahead.

- **Establish Firm Boundaries**: Define clear boundaries to protect your time and energy. Communicate your limits assertively and honor them to maintain a healthy work-life balance, safeguarding your well-being and productivity.

- **Cultivate Authentic Connections**: Lean into your capacity for deep, meaningful relationships. Build genuine connections with clients, collaborators, and mentors who appreciate your introverted strengths and support your entrepreneurial endeavors.

- **Leverage Technology Strategically**: Embrace digital tools and platforms to amplify your brand and expand your reach. Utilize social media and online networking to connect with like-minded individuals and showcase your unique value proposition.

- **Stay Informed and Adaptive**: Keep abreast of industry trends and developments, equipping yourself with the knowledge needed to stay ahead of the curve. Embrace change with agility, leveraging your introspective nature to innovate and pivot as needed.

- **Harness Your Problem-Solving Skills**: Your analytical and reflective approach to problem-solving is a potent asset in business. Embrace challenges as opportunities for creative problem-solving, leveraging your innate ability to find elegant solutions.

- **Refine Your Written Communication**: Enhance your written communication skills to effectively convey your ideas and vision. Clear and concise communication fosters understanding and strengthens your relationships with stakeholders.

- **Embrace Active Listening**: Your attentive listening skills are invaluable in building trust and rapport. Listen deeply to the needs of your clients and collaborators, demonstrating empathy and understanding in your interactions.

- **Strive for Balance**: Create harmony between your professional and personal pursuits. Prioritize self-care, leisure activities, and moments of solitude to recharge and maintain your well-being amidst the demands of entrepreneurship.

- **Seek Meaningful Networking Opportunities**: Engage in smaller, intimate gatherings where you can forge authentic connections. Quality over quantity is key; prioritize events and communities that align with your values and interests.

- **Commit to Continuous Growth**: Embrace self-awareness and a growth mindset on your entrepreneurial journey. Reflect on your experiences, learn from challenges, and invest in your personal and professional development to realize your full potential.

By embracing these tailored tips, you can navigate the entrepreneurial landscape with confidence and authenticity. Your introverted strengths are not limitations but powerful assets that can drive innovation, foster meaningful connections, and propel you toward entrepreneurial success. Embrace your introversion, honor your unique perspective, and let your entrepreneurial spirit soar.

In summary, introverts can navigate extroverted environments by embracing their unique strengths and implementing tailored strategies. Whether thriving in social workplaces or venturing into entrepreneurship, introverts have the power to contribute meaningfully and achieve remarkable success. The journey of introverted entrepreneurs serves as inspiration, illustrating that introversion can be a valuable asset in the dynamic world of work and business.

 **Chapter highlights:**

- By focusing on delivering results, showing potential through skill development and initiative, gaining advocacy through supportive relationships, fostering strong friendships, seeking mentorship, and continuously learning and developing, introverts can navigate their career advancement effectively and achieve success.
- Success in the workplace for introverts is not solely determined by extroverted traits but by the strategic utilization of their inherent strengths and capabilities.
- Introverts can prioritize job roles that align with their strengths and preferences to ensure long-term satisfaction and success in the workplace.
- Contrary to popular belief, introverted individuals have a wide array of career options available to them. There are numerous opportunities where introverts can excel by working independently, focusing deeply on tasks, and making meaningful contributions in their chosen fields.
- When you examine the achievements of renowned introverted entrepreneurs, you see that success in entrepreneurship

transcends personality traits. As you embark on your entrepreneurial journey, invaluable guidance and tips are tailored specifically for introverted individuals seeking success as entrepreneurs. The guidance empowers you to navigate the entrepreneurial landscape with confidence, authenticity, and success.

Chapter 6

Crafting a Workplace Environment Conducive to Introverts

This chapter is tailored for organizations, leaders, managers, team leaders, and colleagues who interact with introverts in the workplace, aiming to cultivate an environment that respects and nurtures their unique traits.

Picture yourself as a trusted ally to an introverted friend entrusted with the task of fostering a space where they can truly flourish. Drawing insights from the sections ahead, let's collaborate to empower introverts and contribute to their professional fulfillment.

In this chapter, we will explore the following key areas: Understanding Introverts' Expectations from others, Strategies for Organizations and Leaders to Facilitate Introverts' Success, Effective Approaches to Managing Introverted Employees, and Practical Tips for Extroverts to Offer Support and Encouragement to Introverts.

Understanding Introverts' Expectations from Others

Introverts are often misconstrued as reserved or aloof, and they possess distinct requirements and hopes in their social interactions. While extroverts draw energy from external stimuli and social engagements, introverts seek solace in solitude and introspection. Unveiling the expectations of introverts can pave the way for enhanced relationships and the cultivation of a more inclusive and supportive environment for all involved.

Craving Space and Solitude

Foremost among introverts' expectations is their desire for personal space and alone time. Introverts replenish their energy reserves through moments of solitude, away from the incessant demands of social engagements. It is imperative for others to acknowledge and honor this need, refraining from taking it personally when introverts seek moments of seclusion. Granting introverts the space they yearn for allows them to recharge and engage more authentically when they do partake in social interactions.

Valuing Deep Conversations

Introverts prize profound, meaningful dialogues over superficial small talk. They cherish active listening and deliberate engagement from their counterparts. Rather than monopolizing discussions, introverts anticipate genuine interest and attentive participation from others. Engaging in conversations that foster introspection and intellectual exchange can make introverts feel appreciated and understood.

Mitigating Overstimulation

Introverts easily become overwhelmed by excessive noise, bustling crowds, and overstimulating environments. They anticipate considerate behavior from others regarding their sensitivity to external stimuli. This entails refraining from subjecting introverts to settings where they feel uncomfortable or depleted, such as raucous parties or bustling gatherings. Offering alternative avenues for social interaction, such as intimate gatherings or one-on-one exchanges, can alleviate introverts' unease.

Respecting Personal Boundaries

Introverts maintain a firm stance on personal boundaries. They expect others to honor their limits and refrain from coercing them into discomforting situations. For instance, introverts may decline social invitations without feeling compelled to furnish detailed justifications. It is vital for others to recognize that introverts thrive when they retain agency over their social interactions and are not coerced into scenarios that sap their energy.

In essence, comprehending introverts' expectations from others serves as a cornerstone for nurturing robust and meaningful relationships. By honoring their need for solitude, engaging in profound conversations, mitigating overstimulation, and respecting their personal boundaries, we can forge an environment that champions and esteems introverts. Embracing the unique attributes of introverts can lead to more enriching and gratifying social exchanges for all parties involved.

Strategies for Organizations and Leaders to Facilitate Introverts' Success

Understanding and accommodating the needs of introverted individuals is crucial for fostering a diverse and inclusive workplace culture. While extroverted personalities may thrive in bustling settings, introverts often excel in quieter, more introspective environments. However, many organizational structures and leadership styles are geared toward extroverted tendencies, inadvertently marginalizing introverted employees. To address this imbalance and promote the success of introverts, organizations, leaders, and employee engagement initiatives can implement a range of strategies tailored to their unique strengths and preferences.

These recommendations cover aspects relating to organizational infrastructure, culture leadership practices and team dynamics.

- **Acknowledge the Introversion-Extroversion Spectrum:** Recognize the varying degrees of introversion and extroversion among individuals and tailor organizational approaches to accommodate these differences, promoting inclusivity.

- **Respect Work Boundaries:** Acknowledge the importance of respecting introverts' work boundaries and providing conducive office spaces tailored to their needs. By recognizing introverts' preference for uninterrupted work time, leaders can foster a supportive culture that values focused productivity over constant interruptions. Integrate designated quiet zones or alternative workspaces within open office layouts, equipped with comfortable seating and minimal distractions, to empower introverts to work efficiently and optimize their well-being. This proactive approach not only enhances productivity but also demonstrates a commitment to creating inclusive workplaces where all employees can thrive.

- **Promote Written Communication:** Actively encourage the utilization of written communication platforms such as emails and messaging tools to empower introverts to express themselves effectively and contribute meaningfully to discussions and projects. Additionally, it provides platforms for introverts to share their ideas and concerns, ensuring their voices are heard and valued within the organization.

- **Offer Flexible Work Arrangements:** Provide introverted individuals with the option for remote work or flexible schedules, allowing them to structure their workdays according to their preferences and energy levels, ultimately boosting job satisfaction and productivity.

- **Enhancing Meeting Practices for Introverts:** Designate Meeting-Free Days to offer introverts uninterrupted time for deep work, boosting their focus and productivity. Additionally, streamline meeting structures by providing advance notice and clear agendas, ensuring effective participation from introverts. Evaluate the necessity of face-to-face meetings and explore alternative communication methods to minimize disruptions and accommodate introverted preferences.

- **Revise Interview Processes:** Modify interview formats to include more one-on-one conversations rather than panel-style interviews, alleviating stress for introverted candidates and allowing them to showcase their abilities more comfortably.

- **Champion Introverted Leadership:** Challenge traditional leadership stereotypes by recognizing and promoting introverted individuals into leadership positions, acknowledging their unique strengths such as thoughtful decision-making and strong listening skills, thereby fostering diversity and inclusivity in leadership roles.

- **Facilitate Social Opportunities:** Create optional social platforms and events where introverts can engage at their own pace and comfort level, promoting connections and networking opportunities without imposing participation requirements.

- **Foster Structured Brainstorming Sessions:** Organize brainstorming sessions with structured formats to accommodate introverts' preferences for thoughtful contributions while also encouraging solo idea generation before group discussions to ensure all voices are heard.

- **Provide Opportunities for Individual Work:** Assign tasks or projects that require focused attention to leverage introverts' strengths while also maintaining smaller team sizes to reduce stress and enhance collaboration, adhering to principles such as Jeff Bezos' two-pizza rule for optimal teamwork.

- **Invest in Tailored Training and Development:** Offer training on understanding different personalities and working styles. Offer on-going training opportunities specifically designed to enhance introverted employees' skills and confidence, demonstrating organizational commitment to their professional growth and success. Areas to consider are public speaking, presentation, and networking skills.

In summary, effectively engaging introverts requires a nuanced approach that recognizes their strengths, respects their preferences, and creates an inclusive work environment. By implementing strategies at both the infrastructure and leadership levels and investing in employee engagement initiatives tailored to introverts, organizations can foster a culture of inclusivity and maximize the potential of their workforce.

Effective Approaches to Managing Introverted Employees

Managers can play a critical role in understanding and accommodating the diverse needs of employees, which is key to fostering a thriving and inclusive environment. Among these considerations, recognizing and supporting introverted employees can significantly contribute to a team's success. While introverts may not always be the loudest voices in the room, their unique strengths and perspectives can greatly enrich the collective efforts of a team when managed effectively. Here are some strategies managers can employ to unlock the full potential of their introverted team members:

Creating a Supportive Work Environment:

- **Ask for Input and Preferences:** Engage introverted employees in discussions about their work preferences, including their preferred communication styles and ideal work environments. By understanding their needs, managers can tailor the workplace to better accommodate introverts' preferences, fostering a more comfortable and productive atmosphere.

- **Assign Work Buddies:** Recognize introverts' inclination toward one-on-one interactions by pairing them with work buddies. This approach allows introverts to collaborate effectively while providing them with the necessary space for recharge and reflection.

Fostering Positive Relationships:

- **Develop a Rapport:** Building strong relationships with introverted employees requires intentional effort. Regular one-on-one meetings provide an opportunity for managers to discuss work-related matters as well as personal goals, fostering a sense of trust and connection.

- **Focus on Strengths:** Acknowledge and leverage introverts' strengths, such as active listening and thoughtful observation, to enhance team dynamics. By highlighting these attributes, managers can empower introverts to contribute meaningfully to team projects.

Supporting Well-being and Performance:

- **Allow Downtime:** Recognize introverts' need for solitude and reflection by providing opportunities for downtime. Incorporating breaks into their schedules allows introverts to recharge after social interactions, promoting sustained high performance.

- **Practice Patience:** Building trust and understanding with introverted employees takes time. Managers should demonstrate patience and commitment to creating a supportive work environment that values introverts' unique contributions.

Effective Communication and Work Practices:

- **Avoid Putting Them on the Spot:** Introverted employees may feel uncomfortable speaking up in group settings. To accommodate their preferences, managers should provide alternative avenues for feedback, such as written submissions or private discussions.

- **Help Them Speak Up:** Encourage introverted employees to participate by providing advance notice for group interactions and creating a culture that values thoughtful contributions. Private discussions can also provide a platform for introverts to share their ideas and perspectives.

Continuous Learning and Development:

- **Educate Yourself:** Take the time to learn about the personalities and preferences of team members, including introverts. This understanding fosters a more unified and peaceful work environment where everyone feels valued and respected.

- **Rethink the Workday:** Consider implementing flexible work options and evaluating the work environment to better accommodate introverts' needs. Providing a variety of work settings and schedules allows introverted employees to thrive in their roles.

Promoting Collaboration and Recognition:

- **Prioritize Team Building:** Create opportunities for team building that accommodate introverts' preferences, such as smaller group activities or team building exercises with clear guidelines and participation options.

- **Encourage Extroverts to Listen:** Foster understanding among extroverted colleagues and promote active listening to respect diverse working styles. By encouraging empathy and inclusivity, managers can create a culture where introverted voices are heard and valued.

In summary, effective management of introverted employees involves creating a supportive work environment, fostering positive relationships, supporting well-being and performance, implementing effective communication practices, promoting continuous learning and development, and prioritizing collaboration and recognition. By embracing these strategies, managers can unlock the full potential of their introverted team members, leading to increased productivity, innovation, and overall team success.

Fostering Introverted Talent: Roshini - a Manager's Journey to Success

Roshini, a team manager, faced the challenge of leading a diverse team with varying personalities and work styles. Among her team members was Sarita, a talented but introverted individual who often preferred solitude over socializing in group settings.

One day, Roshini noticed Sarita sitting quietly at her desk, immersed in her work while her extroverted colleagues engaged in animated discussions. Sensing Sarita's discomfort in the bustling environment, Roshini decided to take proactive steps to support her introverted team member.

Approaching Sarita's desk, Roshini initiated a conversation, "Hey Sarita, I noticed you've been working diligently. How are you finding the team dynamics lately?"

Sarita looked up, surprised by Roshini's genuine interest in her well-being. "It's been a bit overwhelming, to be honest. I sometimes struggle to voice my ideas in group meetings," she confessed.

Listening attentively, Roshini nodded empathetically. "I understand. Everyone has their own preferred communication styles. How about we try something different to ensure your ideas are heard?"

In the following weeks, Roshini implemented several strategies to accommodate Sarita's introverted nature. She assigned Sarita a work buddy, Ankur, who shared similar work preferences. Together, they collaborated effectively on projects, providing each other with the necessary space for recharge and reflection.

Roshini also scheduled regular one-on-one meetings with Sarita to discuss work-related matters and personal goals. These meetings allowed Roshini to develop a rapport with Sarita, building trust and understanding over time.

Recognizing Sarita's strengths in active listening and thoughtful observation, Roshini began highlighting her contributions during team meetings. She encouraged Sarita to share her ideas through alternative avenues, such as written submissions or private discussions.

As Roshini continued to support Sarita's well-being and performance, she noticed a positive shift in the team dynamics. Sarita became more confident in expressing her ideas, and her unique perspective enriched team discussions and project outcomes.

One day, during a brainstorming session, Sarita surprised her colleagues with a brilliant idea that garnered praise from the entire team. Roshini smiled proudly, knowing that her efforts to nurture Sarita's introverted talent had paid off.

Reflecting on their journey together, Roshini realized the importance of embracing diverse personalities in the workplace. By understanding and *accommodating the needs of introverted employees like Sarita, managers could unlock their full potential, leading to increased productivity, innovation, and overall team success.*

Practical Tips for Extroverts to Offer Support and Encouragement to Introverts

Working effectively with introverts involves adopting behaviors that foster understanding, respect, and collaboration. Here is a summary of some insightful suggestions from extroverts on how to create a more comfortable environment for introverts in the workplace.

As a colleague working alongside introverts, it's important for me, as an extrovert, to be mindful of their needs and preferences in the workplace. Here are some behaviors I've adopted to help introverts feel more comfortable:

✓ **Active Listening:** I make a conscious effort to actively listen to introverted colleagues when they're sharing their thoughts or ideas. I give them the time and space they need to express themselves fully without interrupting or dominating the conversation.

✓ **Respect for Personal Space:** I respect their personal space and privacy, understanding that they may need time alone to recharge. I avoid intruding on their workspace or initiating conversations when they seem focused on their tasks.

✓ **Facilitating Small Group Discussions:** Instead of large group settings, I meet them in small group discussions or one-on-one meetings. This creates a more comfortable environment for them to participate and share their ideas.

✓ **Giving Advance Notice:** I make sure to give introverted colleagues advance notice of meetings, events, or changes in plans. This allows them to mentally prepare and reduces any anxiety they may feel about unexpected situations.

✓ **Written Communication:** I use written communication methods, such as emails or instant messaging, knowing that introverts may prefer them over verbal communication. This provides them with alternative channels to express themselves effectively.

✓ **Being Inclusive in Group Activities:** When organizing team activities or social events, I ensure that introverted colleagues feel included and respected. I provide options for participation and respect their boundaries to create a welcoming environment for everyone.

✓ **Avoiding Overwhelming Introverts:** "I'm mindful not to overwhelm introverted colleagues with too much stimuli or constant social interaction. I give them space to recharge and respect their need for quiet time to stay productive."

By adopting these behaviors, I aim to create a supportive and inclusive work environment where introverted colleagues feel valued, respected, and comfortable being themselves. This not only fosters better collaboration but also enhances overall team productivity and morale.

Bridging Extrovert-Introvert Dynamics

In the bustling conference room of a tech start-up, Suresh, the outgoing and energetic project manager, led a brainstorming session with his team. Among them was Rakesh, a talented but introverted software developer who often found himself overshadowed in group settings.

As the discussion gained momentum, Suresh noticed Rakesh sitting quietly, his brow furrowed in concentration as he scribbled notes on his notepad. Sensing Rakesh's hesitation to speak up, Suresh decided to take action.

"Suresh, do you have any thoughts on this?" Suresh turned to Rakesh, breaking the flow of the conversation, and directing the attention toward him.

Rakesh looked up, startled by the sudden focus on him. "Um, well, I was thinking..." he began tentatively, his voice trailing off as he struggled to articulate his ideas.

Suresh smiled encouragingly, nodding his head in support. "Take your time, Rakesh. We're all ears," he reassured, gesturing for the team to give Rakesh the space he needed to gather his thoughts.

Feeling the weight of Suresh's encouragement, Rakesh took a deep breath and began to share his insights. As he spoke, Suresh listened intently, nodding along and occasionally interjecting with words of affirmation.

As the meeting progressed, Suresh made a conscious effort to facilitate small group discussions, ensuring that Rakesh felt comfortable participating. He also gave Rakesh advance notice of upcoming meetings and events, allowing him time to prepare and alleviate any anxiety he may have felt about unexpected situations.

Throughout the discussion, Suresh used written communication methods to supplement verbal discussions, recognizing Rakesh's preference for alternative channels of expression.

As the meeting came to a close, Suresh made a point to include Rakesh in the team's plans for future activities, respecting his boundaries and ensuring that he felt valued and included.

Reflecting on the meeting, Suresh realized the importance of adapting his leadership style to accommodate the diverse needs of his team members. By offering support and encouragement to introverted colleagues like Rakesh, he fostered a more inclusive and collaborative work environment where everyone felt empowered to contribute their ideas and insights.

 **Chapter highlights:**

- Understanding introverts' expectations from others, such as their need for personal space and solitude, preference for deep conversations, sensitivity to overstimulation, and respect for personal boundaries, is essential for nurturing robust and meaningful relationships. By honoring these expectations, individuals can create a more inclusive and supportive environment that values and respects the unique qualities and preferences of introverts.

- Organizations and leaders can support introverted individuals by implementing tailored strategies. These include respecting work boundaries, promoting written communication, offering flexible work arrangements, enhancing meeting practices, championing introverted leadership, fostering structured brainstorming sessions, and providing customized training opportunities. By recognizing and accommodating their needs, organizations can create an inclusive environment where introverts thrive alongside extroverted colleagues.

- Effective management of introverted employees involves creating a supportive work environment, fostering positive relationships, supporting well-being and performance, implementing effective communication practices, promoting continuous learning and development, and prioritizing collaboration and recognition. By embracing these strategies, managers can unlock the full potential of their introverted team members, leading to increased productivity, innovation, and overall team success.

- Extroverts can support introverted colleagues by actively listening, respecting personal space, facilitating small group discussions, giving advance notice, using written communication, being inclusive in group activities, and avoiding overwhelming introverts. By adopting these behaviors, extroverts can create a supportive and inclusive work environment where introverted colleagues feel valued, respected, and comfortable being themselves, leading to better collaboration, productivity, and morale within the team.

Chapter 7

Exploring the Spectrum: Introversion and Extraversion in Psychology and Beyond

Delving into the complexities of human personality, the concepts of introversion and extraversion, emerge as essential orientations that fundamentally influence our interactions, perceptions, and core motivations. Initially introduced by Carl Jung in his ground-breaking theory of psychological types, these orientations have not only influenced the bedrock of personality psychology but have also invited extensive exploration and refinement by numerous scholars and practitioners. This chapter delves into the origins of these concepts within Jung's analytical psychology, their subsequent elaboration by a diverse array of psychologists, and their practical application in tools such as the Myers-Briggs Type Indicator (MBTI). Furthermore, we will explore the nuanced understanding of introversion, revealing the multifaceted nature of introverted personalities. Beyond the realms of Western psychology, Indian scriptures and scholars offer rich insights that resonate with these concepts, providing a unique cultural perspective on the inner workings of the introverted and extroverted orientations. This convergence of ideas from Western psychological theories and Eastern philosophical teachings presents a comprehensive backdrop against which the intricacies of introversion and extraversion can be understood, offering a multidimensional view of these complex personality orientations.

Carl Jung's theory of psychological types

The term "introvert" was popularized by Carl Jung in the early 20th century. He was a Swiss psychiatrist and psychoanalyst who founded analytical psychology and proposed a complex theory of personality in which he described various psychological types. In his psychological typology, Jung described introverts as individuals who tend to turn their energy and attention inward, focusing on their own thoughts, feelings, and reflections. Jung contrasted introverts with extraverts, who direct their energy outward, engaging more actively with the external world and the people in it. Although the concept of introversion existed before Jung, his work was instrumental in defining and disseminating the term as it is understood in psychology today.

Carl Jung's theory of psychological types is a foundational aspect of analytical psychology, offering a rich framework for understanding the complexities of human personality. His theory is multifaceted, emphasizing the interplay of conscious and unconscious processes in shaping personality. Here are the key components of Jung's theory:

Psychological Attitudes: Introversion and Extraversion

- **Introversion**: Characterized by an inward focus of energy on subjective experiences, thoughts, and feelings. Introverts are more concerned with their internal world and personal reflections.
- **Extraversion**: Marked by an outward focus of energy on external events, interactions, and the objective world.

Extraverts are more engaged with external stimuli and social activities.

Psychological Functions

Jung identified four primary psychological functions that influence how individuals perceive the world and make decisions. These functions are divided into two perceiving (or irrational) functions and two judging (or rational) functions:

- **Thinking**: A judging function that involves making decisions based on logical analysis and objective principles.
- **Feeling**: Another judging function, but decisions are based on subjective values and emotional responses.
- **Sensing**: A perceiving function that involves obtaining information through the direct sensory experience of the physical world.
- **Intuition**: Also a perceiving function, but it focuses on perceiving patterns, possibilities, and abstract meanings beyond immediate sensory data.

Each individual has a dominant function, which plays a primary role in their personality, and an auxiliary function that supports and balances the dominant one.

The Collective Unconscious and Archetypes

- **Collective Unconscious**: A universal level of the unconscious shared by all humans, containing archetypes and instincts inherited from our ancestors.
- **Archetypes**: Universal, symbolic images and themes that recur across cultures and time periods, residing in the collective unconscious. Examples include the Persona (the mask one wears in public), the Shadow (repressed or denied aspects of

the self), the Anima and Animus (the feminine aspect in males and the masculine aspect in females, respectively), and the Self (the unification of consciousness and unconsciousness in an individual, representing the psyche as a whole).

The Process of Individuation

Jung's concept of individuation is the process of becoming aware of oneself and integrating the conscious and unconscious parts of the psyche. This process involves recognizing and reconciling opposites within the personality, such as the conscious and unconscious, introversion and extraversion, and the various psychological functions. The goal of individuation is the development of the Self, leading to a more harmonious and balanced personality.

Synchronicity

Jung also introduced the concept of synchronicity, a principle of acausal connection. Synchronicity suggests that events are meaningfully related not by cause and effect but through their symbolic significance to the individual. This concept emphasizes the interplay between the inner and outer worlds.

Carl Jung's theory has profoundly influenced psychology, psychotherapy, art, literature, and spiritual and cultural studies. His work laid the groundwork for understanding the complexities of personality and the importance of integrating various aspects of the psyche for psychological health and personal growth.

Jung believed that everyone has both an introverted and an extraverted side, with one being more dominant than the other. Introversion, in Jung's view, is characterized by an orientation of energy toward the inner world of thoughts, feelings, and reflections, whereas extraversion is oriented toward the external world of activities and social interactions.

Others

Beyond Carl Jung, several other psychologists and researchers have significantly contributed to the understanding and development of theories related to introversion and extraversion. Some of the most notable figures include:

- **Hans Eysenck**: Eysenck was a German-British psychologist known for his work on personality and intelligence. He proposed a biological basis for personality traits, suggesting that differences in the reticular activation system (RAS) could explain the variance between introverts and extroverts. According to Eysenck, introverts have higher levels of baseline cortical arousal, making them more sensitive to stimulation, while extroverts have lower levels, leading them to seek out more stimulation.

- **Jerome Kagan**: An American psychologist, Kagan conducted extensive research on temperament in children. He identified two types of temperaments that are somewhat analogous to introversion and extraversion: inhibited and uninhibited temperaments. Kagan's research suggested that these temperaments are evident from infancy and are influenced by inherited physiological characteristics.

- **Jonathan Cheek**: A psychologist known for his research on shyness and introversion, Cheek has contributed to understanding the nuances within introversion. He and his colleagues have proposed the distinction between four subtypes of introversion: social, thinking, anxious, and restrained, offering a more detailed view of introverted personality beyond the traditional dichotomy of introversion-extraversion.

These individuals, among others, have expanded our understanding of introversion and extraversion from various perspectives, including biological, developmental, and sociocultural viewpoints. Their work has contributed to a more nuanced and complex view of these personality traits, recognizing the diversity within the categories of introversion and extraversion themselves.

MBTI – applying Carl Jung's theory

The Myers-Briggs Type Indicator (MBTI) is directly influenced by Carl Jung's theory of psychological types. Katharine Cook Briggs and her daughter Isabel Briggs Myers developed the MBTI with the goal of making Jung's theory understandable and useful in people's lives. The MBTI shares several core concepts with Jung's theory, particularly the emphasis on introversion and extraversion as fundamental orientations and the identification of functions that describe how people perceive the world and make decisions. Here are the key similarities between Jung's theory and the MBTI:

- **Introversion and Extraversion**: Both systems recognize these as opposite orientations of energy. In Jung's theory, introversion involves an inward focus on thoughts and feelings, while extraversion involves an outward focus on the external world and interactions. The MBTI incorporates this distinction as one of its primary dichotomies.

- **Psychological Functions**: Jung identified four primary psychological functions: thinking, feeling, sensing, and intuition. He also distinguished between introverted and extroverted orientations of these functions. The MBTI builds on this foundation, using these functions to create 16 distinct personality types. Each type is described by a four-letter code that indicates whether a person is more introverted (I) or extroverted (E), sensing (S) or intuitive (N), thinking (T) or feeling (F), and judging (J) or perceiving (P).

- **Dominant and Auxiliary Functions**: Jung's concept of dominant and auxiliary functions, where one function is primary, and another serves to support it, is also foundational to the MBTI. Each of the 16 MBTI types has a dominant function (either a perceiving function like sensing or intuition or a judging function like thinking or feeling) and an auxiliary function that helps to balance the dominant one.

- **Type Dynamics**: Both Jung's theory and the MBTI suggest that individuals have a natural preference for how they perceive information and make decisions, leading to different ways of interacting with the world. The MBTI expands on Jung's ideas by suggesting how these preferences interact dynamically within each personality type, influencing behavior, relationships, and personal growth.

The main difference between Jung's original theory and the MBTI is in its structure and application. Jung's descriptions of psychological types were more theoretical and focused on a broad understanding of personality dynamics. The MBTI, on the other hand, operationalizes these concepts into a specific assessment tool designed to help people understand their own and others' preferences in perception and decision-making.

The MBTI serves as a direct application of Jung's theory, designed to facilitate personal development, career planning, team building, and a deeper understanding of interpersonal differences. Its creation was driven by the aim to make Jung's complex insights both accessible and practical for everyday use. This tool empowers individuals to better understand themselves and others, thereby improving interpersonal relationships and informing decisions related to career paths and life choices.

The MBTI identifies 16 personality types based on four dichotomies, which represent preferences in how people perceive the world and make decisions:

- **Introversion (I) or Extraversion (E)**: This dimension aligns with Jung's original concept, indicating the direction of a person's energy and attention—either inward toward thoughts and feelings (Introversion) or outward toward people and activities (Extraversion).

- **Sensing (S) or Intuition (N)**: This preference indicates whether a person primarily focuses on the actual, present information received through the senses (Sensing) or prefers to interpret and add meaning, focusing on patterns, possibilities, and abstract concepts (Intuition).

- **Thinking (T) or Feeling (F)**: This dichotomy shows whether a person tends to make decisions based on objective principles and logical analysis (Thinking) or is more influenced by personal values and considerations about the impact on others (Feeling).

- **Judging (J) or Perceiving (P)**: This preference indicates whether a person likes to live in a more structured, decided way (Judging) or prefers to stay open to new information and options, adopting a more flexible and adaptable approach (Perceiving).

Each of the 16 personality types is denoted by a four-letter code that represents the individual's preferences in these four dichotomies. The MBTI assumes that these preferences are innate and relatively stable over time, forming the basis of one's personality.

The MBTI has been widely used in various settings, including organizational development, career counseling, education, and personal development. While it has faced criticism regarding its scientific validity and reliability, it remains popular as a tool for self-discovery and team building, largely due to its practical applications and the insightful framework it offers for understanding and appreciating personality differences.

Types of Introversion as per MBTI

MBTI identifies eight introverted types based on their dominant cognitive function, which operates primarily in an inward-focused manner. Each of these types combines introversion with one of the four cognitive functions (Thinking, Feeling, Sensing, Intuition), further distinguished by whether the function is used in a more perceiving or judging manner. The eight introverted types in the MBTI are as follows:

- **ISTJ**: Dominant introverted sensing (Si) with auxiliary extroverted thinking (Te). ISTJs are practical and reliable, and they focus on details and facts from past experiences.
- **ISFJ**: Dominant introverted sensing (Si) with auxiliary extroverted feeling (Fe). ISFJs are nurturing, detail-oriented, and dedicated, often focusing on providing support and care based on past experiences.
- **INFJ**: Dominant introverted intuition (Ni) with auxiliary extroverted feeling (Fe). INFJs are insightful, empathetic, and driven by a sense of purpose, often focused on future possibilities and human potential.
- **INTJ**: Dominant introverted intuition (Ni) with auxiliary extroverted thinking (Te). INTJs are strategic, analytical, and innovative, often focused on future possibilities and efficient solutions.

- **ISTP**: Dominant introverted thinking (Ti) with auxiliary extroverted sensing (Se). ISTPs are adaptable, skilful, and independent, often excelling in problem-solving and hands-on tasks.
- **ISFP**: Dominant introverted feeling (Fi) with auxiliary extroverted sensing (Se). ISFPs are sensitive, creative, and in tune with their values, often expressing themselves through practical actions and aesthetics.
- **INFP**: Dominant introverted feeling (Fi) with auxiliary extroverted intuition (Ne). INFPs are idealistic, empathetic, and creative, often focused on exploring possibilities and personal values.
- **INTP**: Dominant introverted thinking (Ti) with auxiliary extroverted intuition (Ne). INTPs are analytical, curious, and innovative, often focused on exploring theories and abstract concepts.

Each of these types of experiences and expresses introversion differently, depending on their dominant function and how it interacts with their auxiliary function. This diversity within introverted types highlights the nuanced ways in which individuals engage with their inner world and process information.

Similarly, the eight extroverted types in the MBTI are as follows:

- **ESTP**: Action-oriented, pragmatic, and adaptable, excelling in situations that require quick thinking and responsiveness to immediate sensory information.
- **ESFP**: Outgoing, friendly, and enthusiastic, thriving in environments that allow them to engage actively with people and their surroundings.

- **ENFP**: Imaginative, warm, and spontaneous, driven by a desire to explore possibilities and connect with others on a deep level.
- **ENTP**: Inventive, curious, and adaptable, often drawn to exploring new ideas and engaging in intellectual debates.
- **ESTJ**: Organized, decisive, and practical, excelling in leadership roles that require clear direction and adherence to established structures.
- **ESFJ**: Sociable, caring, and conscientious, often focused on creating harmony and supporting others within their community.
- **ENFJ**: Empathetic, persuasive, and forward-looking, motivated by a desire to understand others and help them realize their potential.
- **ENTJ**: Strategic, ambitious, and assertive, skilled at planning and executing projects with a clear vision of the future.

Indian scriptures

Indian scriptures, spanning a vast array of philosophical, spiritual, and religious texts, do not directly categorize human behavior in terms of modern psychological concepts like introversion and extroversion. However, they do delve into understanding different personality types, temperaments, and paths to spiritual growth that can relate to what we understand today as introverted and extroverted behaviors.

Bhagavad Gita: In the Bhagavad Gita, which is part of the epic Mahabharata, a conversation between Prince Arjuna and his charioteer, Lord Krishna, various paths to spiritual realization are discussed, reflecting different temperaments and behaviors. For example, the path of knowledge (Jnana Yoga) might appeal more to introspective or introverted individuals who seek understanding through meditation and contemplation. In contrast, the path of action (Karma Yoga) might resonate more with extroverted individuals, emphasizing selfless service and active engagement in the world. The Bhagavad Gita discusses the concept of "Sattva," "Rajas," and "Tamas," which are qualities (gunas) present in all individuals. These qualities can offer some insights into introverted and extroverted behaviors:

- **Sattva** is purity, knowledge, and harmony. Individuals with a predominant Sattva may exhibit introverted qualities such as being calm, introspective, and focused on inner peace and knowledge.
- **Rajas** are passion, activity, and restlessness. Rajasic individuals might display extroverted qualities like being energetic and ambitious and seeking external activities and engagement.
- **Tamas** is darkness, ignorance, and inertia. Tamasic behavior could manifest in withdrawal and laziness, which might superficially resemble introversion but comes from a place of ignorance rather than a desire for introspection.

Sankhya Philosophy: Sankhya, one of the six schools of Indian philosophy, analyses the mind and consciousness in detail. It describes various elements of the psyche (e.g., mind, ego, and intellect) and how they interact with the material and spiritual worlds. This analytical approach can offer insights into different personality traits, possibly aligning with introverted and extroverted behaviors through the lens of how individuals interact with their inner and outer environments.

Ayurveda: Ayurveda, the traditional Indian system of medicine, categorizes individuals based on three doshas (biological energies): Vata, Pitta, and Kapha. While not directly equivalent to introversion and extroversion, these doshas describe physical, emotional, and mental characteristics that influence behavior and health. Each person has a unique balance of these doshas, affecting their physical health, behavior, and emotions. Understanding one's predominant dosha can also offer insights into one's natural tendencies toward introversion or extroversion:

- **Vata** (air and space) individuals might be seen as creative and energetic with fluctuating moods, resembling a combination of extroverted and introverted qualities.
- **Pitta** (fire and water) personalities may be ambitious and driven, with a mixture of introverted and extroverted tendencies depending on the context.
- **Kapha** (earth and water) individuals are often calm, steady, and content, which could be aligned with introverted characteristics.

Yoga Sutras of Patanjali: The Yoga Sutras of Patanjali, a foundational text on the path to spiritual realization through yoga, emphasizes practices such as self-study (Svadhyaya) and meditation (Dhyana). While these concepts do not explicitly address introversion or extroversion, they offer valuable insights for those inclined toward introspection and solitude, often associated with introverted individuals. The text outlines Raja Yoga, a disciplined approach to achieving spiritual insight and liberation, focusing on mastering the mind and senses. This inward journey may resonate particularly with introverts, fostering inner peace and self-awareness. However, the principles of yoga, including its ethical precepts (Yamas and Niyamas), offer universal benefits, supporting personal growth and well-being across all personality types.

Upanishads: The Upanishads, ancient philosophical texts that explore the nature of reality and the self, contain discussions on meditation, self-inquiry, and the search for inner truth. These themes resonate with the introspective nature often attributed to introverts.

Jain and Buddhist Texts: Jainism and Buddhism, which originated in ancient India, emphasize practices such as mindfulness, meditation, and self-awareness. These traditions encourage individuals to look inward, contemplate their thoughts and actions, and cultivate inner peace, qualities that align with introverted tendencies.

While these scriptures and systems do not classify people as introverted or extroverted, they acknowledge the diversity of human temperaments and suggest paths suitable for different individuals. They promote a holistic understanding of personality, emphasizing balance, self-awareness, and spiritual growth that transcends simple categorizations.

Indian Scholars

Indian scholars have made notable contributions to the understanding of personality psychology, delving into aspects that, while not always directly linked to introversion and extroversion, enrich the global discourse on personality dynamics and individual differences.

Mysore Narasimhachar Srinivas is a pivotal figure in this realm, primarily as a sociologist whose research extensively covered the caste system, social stratification, and the process of social change in India. His concept of "Sanskritization" provides a lens through which to view individual and group aspirations, social mobility, and the ways these dynamics influence personality and behavior within structured social hierarchies. While Srinivas's work is not explicitly cantered on personality psychology, his insights into social structures and norms offer a valuable context for understanding how societal factors can shape personality traits, including tendencies toward introversion or extroversion.

Sudhir Kakar is another eminent Indian psychologist whose work intersects with psychoanalysis, culture, and social psychology. Kakar explored the Indian psyche through various lenses, including sexuality, identity, and religion. His books and research offer a psychoanalytic perspective on Indian cultural norms and personal identity, shedding light on the formation of personality in the context of Indian familial and societal structures. Kakar's work suggests how cultural narratives and familial relationships contribute to the development of personality traits, providing a backdrop against which the nuances of introversion and extroversion can be examined.

Ashis Nandy, a political psychologist and social theorist, has contributed significantly to discussions on culture, modernity, and the postcolonial state. Nandy's work, which often critiques the impact of colonialism on identity and psyche, also touches upon how power dynamics and cultural shifts affect individual and collective personalities. His analyses offer insights into how external socio-political pressures and historical contexts shape personal behaviors and traits, including aspects of introversion and extroversion, in subtle yet profound ways.

The contributions of these scholars, while diverse in focus, collectively highlight the importance of considering cultural, social, and historical factors in the study of personality. Their work highlights that personality traits like introversion and extroversion cannot be fully understood in isolation from the societal and cultural contexts that influence individual development. Contemporary Indian psychologists and researchers continue to build on this foundation, employing both empirical methods and theoretical analyses to explore the multifaceted nature of personality in relation to Indian and broader global contexts. These on-going contributions not only enrich the field of personality psychology but also emphasize the need for a multidisciplinary approach to understanding the complexities of human nature.

Chapter highlights:

- Carl Jung's theory of psychological types distinguishes between introversion and extraversion, representing an individual's energy orientation toward either the inner world of thoughts and feelings (introversion) or the external world of activities and social interactions (extraversion). Jung's theory also encompasses other key components such as psychological functions, the collective unconscious and archetypes, the process of individuation, and the concept of synchronicity.

- The contributions of other psychologists like Hans Eysenck, Jerome Kagan, and Jonathan Cheek have further enriched our understanding of introversion and extraversion, offering insights from biological, developmental, and sociocultural perspectives.

- The MBTI is heavily influenced by Carl Jung's theory. MBTI operationalizes Jung's concepts into a practical tool for understanding personality preferences in perception and decision-making. It identifies 16 distinct personality types based on four dichotomies: introversion/extraversion, sensing/intuition, thinking/feeling, and judging/perceiving. While Jung's theory offers a theoretical framework for understanding personality dynamics, the MBTI serves as an accessible and useful application in personal development, career planning, and team building. MBTI is popular for its insightful framework for appreciating personality differences and improving interpersonal relationships.

- Indian scriptures, while not explicitly categorizing human behavior in terms of introversion and extroversion, offer valuable insights into different personality types, temperaments, and paths to spiritual growth. Concepts such as "Sattva," "Rajas," and "Tamas" in the Bhagavad Gita, the doshas in Ayurveda, and practices outlined in texts like the Yoga Sutras of Patanjali and the Upanishads resonate with traits associated with introversion and extroversion. These scriptures promote self-awareness, balance, and spiritual growth, emphasizing the diversity of human temperaments and suggesting paths suitable for different individuals.

- Indian scholars like M.N. Srinivas, Sudhir Kakar, and Ashis Nandy have made significant contributions to understanding personality dynamics within the cultural and social contexts of India. Their work highlights the influence of societal factors on personality traits and underscores the need for a multidisciplinary approach to studying human nature.

SECTION 3

Conclusion

In this concluding section of the book INTROVATIVE, we embark on a reflective journey of introspection and empowerment. Starting with a concise SWOT analysis designed for introverts, you will uncover your core strengths, acknowledge weaknesses, seize opportunities, and recognize potential threats that are unique to your introverted nature. Following this, Maya's story of introverted triumphs awaits to inspire and illustrate the power of leveraging your introverted qualities in the workplace. We then summarize the seven pivotal steps detailed throughout this book, distilling essential insights to arm you with effective strategies and tools for career success. Together, let's embrace our introvert strengths as we wrap up this transformative journey with empowering closing thoughts, ready to thrive in our professional lives.

A brief SWOT Analysis of an Introvert

In conclusion, let me summarize the high-level SWOT analysis of an Introvert.

Strengths:

- Deep Thinkers: Introverts tend to be introspective and thoughtful, often delving into complex issues with depth and clarity.
- Listening Skills: They excel in listening attentively, understanding nuances, and empathizing with others' perspectives.
- Creativity: Many introverts are creative individuals, finding inspiration in solitude and quiet reflection.
- Attention to Detail: They often possess a keen eye for detail, noticing subtleties that others may overlook.
- Independence: Introverts are comfortable working alone and can thrive in environments where they have autonomy and freedom.

Weaknesses:

- Social Interaction: Introverts may struggle in highly social situations, feeling drained or overwhelmed by extensive interaction.
- Assertiveness: They may find it challenging to assert themselves in group settings, preferring to observe rather than take charge.
- Networking: Building connections and networking may be more challenging for introverts who are less inclined to initiate social interactions.
- Public Speaking: Speaking in front of large audiences can be intimidating for introverts, leading to potential discomfort or anxiety.
- Need for Solitude: Introverts may require more alone time to recharge, which could be perceived as withdrawing from team activities or social events.

Opportunities:

- Specialized Roles: Introverts can excel in roles that require deep focus, analysis, and independent work, such as research, writing, or programming.
- Networking Strategies: With tailored networking strategies and opportunities for one-on-one interactions, introverts can build meaningful connections.
- Training and Development: Providing training in communication skills, public speaking, and networking can empower introverts to thrive in various professional settings.
- Flexible Work Environments: Remote work or flexible schedules can accommodate introverts' need for solitude and deep focus, enhancing productivity and job satisfaction.

- Leadership Roles: Introverts can leverage their strengths in listening, empathy, and strategic thinking to excel as leaders, fostering a collaborative and inclusive work culture.

Threats:

- Misunderstanding: Misconceptions about introversion may lead to undervaluing their contributions or misinterpreting their reserved demeanor as disinterest or aloofness.
- Overlooked Opportunities: In environments that prioritize extroverted traits, introverts may miss out on career advancement or leadership roles.
- Social Pressure: Pressure to conform to extroverted norms in social or professional settings can cause stress and discomfort for introverts.
- Communication Barriers: Difficulties in expressing thoughts or ideas verbally may hinder introverts' ability to fully contribute in team meetings or collaborative projects.
- Burnout: Over-exertion in social or high-stimulation environments without adequate rest or recharge time can lead to burnout and decreased job satisfaction for introverts.

Introvert Triumphs: Finding Strength in Maya's Journey

In the bustling heart of the city, amidst the towering skyscrapers and the ceaseless hum of activity, there lived a young introvert named Maya. Despite the vibrant energy that surrounded her, Maya often found solace in the quiet corners of her own mind, where her thoughts roamed free, and her creativity flourished.

In the early days of her career, Maya struggled to navigate the fast-paced world of the workplace. Networking events felt like daunting obstacle courses, and team meetings seemed like battlegrounds where only the loudest voices were heard. Yet, beneath her quiet exterior, Maya harbored a fierce determination to succeed on her own terms.

As Maya embarked on her journey of self-discovery, she encountered challenges and setbacks that tested her resolve. She grappled with self-doubt and wrestled with impostor syndrome, wondering if she truly belonged in a world that seemed tailor-made for extroverts. But with each obstacle she faced, Maya emerged stronger and more resilient, tapping into the depths of her introverted strengths to overcome adversity.

Through introspection and self-reflection, Maya learned to embrace her introverted nature as a source of power rather than a limitation. She discovered the value of her thoughtful insights and her ability to listen deeply to others. Armed with newfound confidence, Maya began to assert herself more assertively in the workplace, advocating for her ideas and contributing her unique perspective to team projects.

As Maya's career progressed, she found herself drawn to leadership roles where she could lead by example and inspire others to embrace their own introverted strengths. She cultivated a supportive network of like-minded individuals who valued her authenticity and respected her quiet leadership style.

Today, Maya stands tall as a beacon of hope for introverts everywhere, proving that success in the workplace is not reserved solely for the extroverted. Through perseverance and determination, Maya has forged a path of her own, paving the way for future generations of introverts to thrive in a world that celebrates their unique talents and contributions.

Closing thoughts: Embracing Your Introvert Power in the Workplace

Reflecting on your journey through introversion is like weaving together insights and discoveries that have shaped your path. You've moved between moments of self-awareness and professional ambition while navigating the dynamic world of work. Along the way, you've explored introspective valleys and reached professional heights. Your adventure has showcased the resilience of the human spirit, guiding you to self-awareness amid the vibrancy of the workplace.

At the core of your exploration lies a simple question resonating in your mind: Is this path truly yours to tread? It's a whisper that prompts you to delve into your innermost self and embrace your introverted nature.

In your pursuit of understanding, you've delved into the essence of introversion, uncovering hidden strengths waiting to be unleashed. Through challenges, you've forged resilience fueled by determination and resolve.

Standing at the threshold of opportunity, you're called to step beyond comfort and embrace adventure. With each stride, you harness introverted strengths, fueling confidence within.

Yet, your journey continues beyond these words, inviting exploration and seizing opportunities ahead. As you bid farewell to this chapter, carry wisdom forward, prepared for the journey ahead. Within introversion's whispers lies the strength to illuminate your path and the courage to navigate life's twists and turns.

Summarizing the Seven Steps – the Key Takeaways:

1. Self-awareness and Acceptance: Understanding your introverted nature and embracing it as a source of strength is foundational to success. By acknowledging your natural tendencies and preferences, you can leverage your unique qualities to excel in your roles.

2. Confidence Building: Cultivating confidence is essential for you to assert yourself effectively in the workplace. Through self-

assurance and positive self-talk, you can overcome self-doubt and step confidently into leadership roles.

3. Effective Communication: Developing effective communication strategies tailored to your introverted style is key. From mastering the art of small talk to assertiveness techniques and public speaking skills, honing your communication abilities enables you to convey your ideas and influence others more persuasively.

4. Networking and Relationship Building: Building meaningful connections with colleagues and stakeholders is vital for your career advancement. You can thrive in networking settings by focusing on quality over quantity and leveraging your listening skills to forge authentic relationships.

5. Collaboration and Teamwork: Excelling in teamwork requires you to leverage your strengths in collaboration while navigating challenges such as group dynamics and assertiveness. By valuing diverse perspectives and fostering open communication, you can contribute effectively to team success.

6. Leadership Development: Cultivating leadership skills tailored to your introverted strengths is essential for aspiring introvert leaders. From prioritizing self-care to leading meetings with confidence and inspiring high-performing teams, you can lead authentically while staying true to your nature.

7. Long-Term Success Strategies: Sustaining success as an introvert involves setting personal and professional goals, developing a career growth plan, and prioritizing self-care. Understanding your energy dynamics, creating an ideal work environment, and advocating for your introvert needs are critical for long-term fulfillment and achievement.

By embracing these key themes and integrating them into your professional journey, you can unlock your full potential and thrive in the dynamic landscape of the workplace.

Harnessing Introvert Power: Final Words

Dear Reader,

As we turn the final pages of INTROVATIVE, let's take a moment to contemplate the profound insights gleaned from each chapter. Each narrative embarked on a path familiar to many introverts – a path often clouded by misconceptions and underestimated potential. Yet, within these pages lies a testament to the inherent strength of introversion.

The impetus behind penning this book was to empower fellow introverts to stride confidently toward their career aspirations. Recognizing the diverse approaches introverts bring to every aspect of life – from operations to communication – I sought to challenge the misconception that our traits equate to slow pace or timidity. Instead, I believe that by embracing select extroverted behaviors while remaining authentic to our core, introverts can propel their professional growth and thrive in the workplace.

INTROVATIVE serves as a toolkit for introverts, equipping them with the knowledge, skills, and strategies essential to navigate the complexities of today's work environment. Through practical insights and actionable advice, it endeavors to foster deeper self-awareness, overcome obstacles, and foster success in both professional and personal realms.

Reflecting on the objectives of this book, I trust that it has provided valuable insights tailored to the needs of introverts:

- Empowering through self-awareness and acceptance, fostering confidence and resilience.
- Navigating workplace challenges by addressing communication, networking, and leadership hurdles.
- Encouraging boldness by guiding introverts through comfort zone expansion and the cultivation of essential interpersonal and leadership skills.
- Identifying avenues for seizing opportunities in diverse career paths, entrepreneurship, and business ventures.
- Advocating for inclusivity, promoting workplace cultures that embrace introversion, collaboration, and holistic well-being.

To all the introverts navigating the maze of the workforce, know that your qualities are indispensable. Embrace your introversion as a wellspring of insight, thoughtfulness, and vision. In a world enamored with loudness and immediacy, remember the immeasurable power of soft reflection, deep understanding, and the persistent pursuit of knowledge.

Your journey is profound. It serves as a testament to the notion that success isn't measured by the volume of your voice but by the depth and sincerity of your actions. Your introverted nature is not a mere facet of your being; it is a gift – to you, your workplace, and the world.

Should you wish to delve deeper into personal development or seek guidance on your professional journey, do not hesitate to reach out. As a coach, I am here to help you unlock your full potential and navigate the complexities of the modern workplace.

As you embark on your own odyssey, armed with newfound knowledge and confidence, remember that your Introvert strength is a force to be reckoned with. Embrace it, nurture it, and let it illuminate your path.

As we embrace our unique strengths and chart our course in the professional realm, may we inspire and uplift fellow introverts on their journey to success.

With warm regards,
Rohit R Chowdhry

About the Author

Rohit R Chowdhry is a full-time Coach, Consultant and Creative Catalyst.

He is a seasoned professional with over three decades of enriching corporate experience. During his 18-year tenure at Deloitte, he held transformative leadership roles, spearheading offshore business operations supporting global clients across various sectors, including professional services and shared services. Widely recognized for his strategic foresight and operational expertise, Rohit has consistently demonstrated his ability to lead large teams across various domains. His areas of focus include business development, seamless transitions, team establishment, meticulous service delivery, performance management, efficiency enhancement, and ensuring adherence to rigorous standards of risk and compliance.

As an accomplished author, Rohit penned the insightful book "How to Get into Your Goldilocks Zone," which offers a roadmap for individuals seeking to maximize their potential and achieve personal and professional fulfillment. His coaching philosophy is deeply rooted in his corporate background and reinforced by his certification as an International Coaching Federation (ICF) coach. Rohit specializes in mid- to senior-level professionals discover their purpose, navigate career transitions, and foster personal development.

Beyond coaching, Rohit is actively involved in training, consulting, and campus engagement initiatives. He designs and delivers leadership and management programs, provides executive coaching to cultivate a culture of innovation, offers consulting services to enhance strategic and operational excellence for organizations, and bridges the gap between academia and the corporate world through campus engagement activities.

In addition to his coaching practice, Rohit is a prolific writer and speaker, sharing his expertise and insights through articles, books, and speaking engagements. He leverages his creative talents in art-infused coaching, using art as a catalyst for deeper personal insights and transformative results. Through customized art-based workshops and a gallery of artworks, Rohit facilitates exploration and connection with art that resonates with individuals' aesthetic sensibilities.

Rohit's multifaceted approach to coaching and consulting, coupled with his diverse skill set as a Consultant, Coach, Trainer, Facilitator, Speaker, Author, and Creative Catalyst, reflects his unwavering commitment to helping individuals and organizations unlock their full potential and thrive in today's dynamic business environment.

You can connect with him on his website, www.rohitrchowdhry.com, where his other social media links are also provided. Scan the QR code to go to his website.

www.ingramcontent.com/pod-product-compliance
Lightning Source LLC
Chambersburg PA
CBHW051146130726

47988CB00005B/2013